Put Your Dreams to Work

*Proven Strategies for Achieving Success
in Your Work and Personal Life*

Annabel Chotzen

PUT YOUR DREAMS TO WORK

Proven Strategies for Achieving Success
in Your Work and Personal Life

Published by: Kukui Publishing

Annabel Chotzen
annabel@annabelchotzen.com
www.annabelchotzen.com
808-728-3355

ISBN: 978-0-578-78225-6
Library of Congress Control Number: 2020920747

Editors: Tyler Tichelaar of Superior Book Productions, Amy Takemoto, and Will Hartzell
Cover and Interior Layout Design: Mirko Pohle
Author Photo: Will Hartzell

Every attempt has been made to properly source all quotes and retell stories as recalled by the author.

Printed in the United States of America
First Edition
2 4 6 8 10 12

To David & Sam,

May all your
dreams come true.

Aloha,
Annabel

DEDICATION

This book is dedicated to those I love and cherish with all my heart and soul:

- Devin Makana Chotzen-Hartzell, my son and greatest teacher

- Will Hartzell, my wonderful husband who has helped make my dreams come true

- My parents, Walter and Carla Chotzen, who encouraged me to follow my dreams

- Allie Diehl, who believed in my dreams and the power of prayer

- Clyde Ikeda, who helped me tell my stories

- Peggy Hartzell, the best mother-in-law in the world

- My seven brothers and sisters: Daniel, Vonny, Claudia, Loren, Vera, Tamar, and Benjamin

ACKNOWLEDGMENTS

Many thanks to those who helped make this book a reality:

Gail Honda

Amy Takemoto

Will Hartzell

Cynthia Wessendorf

Patrick Snow

Nancy Hanson

Marc Beauchamp

May you manifest your greatest dreams
and have an abundant, healthy, happy life.
— Annabel Chotzen

CONTENTS

Introduction

Chapter 1   1
Opening the Gates

Chapter 2   13
Handling Change in Challenging Times

Chapter 3   19
The Platinum Rule

Chapter 4   23
Listening to Other People

Chapter 5   29
Understanding Different Personalities

Chapter 6   37
Resolving Conflict

Chapter 7   49
Communication Effectiveness

Chapter 8   55
The Power to Manifest Your Dreams

Chapter 9   63
The Hawaii Kukui Nut Celebration

Chapter 10   67
Follow Your Joy

Chapter 11   73
Deciding to Live

Chapter 12   77
Moving Your Naha Stone

Chapter 13   87
Connecting and Disconnecting

Chapter 14   91
Discovering the Authentic You

Chapter 15   97
Helping to Fulfill Others' Dreams

Chapter 16   101
Spiritual Guides Help Us

Chapter 17   105
Overcoming Hardships

Chapter 18   113
Healing Your Relationships

Chapter 19   117
Following Your Dreams Despite Setbacks

Chapter 20   125
Pushing Through Fear

Chapter 21   129
Gratitude Brings Dreams Closer

Chapter 22   133
The Importance of a Support Group

Chapter 23   141
Enjoying the Dreams You Are Living Today

Chapter 24   147
When the Dream Changes Form

Chapter 25   151
Nurturing Yourself

Chapter 26   155
My Dream of Becoming a Motivational Speaker

Chapter 27   165
Helping People Go Through the Gates

A Final Thought: The Fulfillment of My Dream   168

About the Author   170

Invite Annabel to Provide Speaking, Coaching,   172
Training, and Consulting Services

INTRODUCTION

Many people die with their dreams still inside of them. Perhaps they were afraid to take a leap into the unknown or were in denial, convincing themselves that "things will get better if I'm patient" or "I don't have what it takes."

Life is an incredible gift. We only have a finite amount of time on this earth. To live an unfulfilled life would be extremely sad. I believe we should be guided by our own inner joy as we pursue what we really want in this lifetime.

Are you a person who has unfulfilled dreams? Is there a desire or yearning inside of you to accomplish something wonderful that would be deeply satisfying?

Have you been holding back because of your own insecurities, or have you been remaining in a relationship or situation because it feels safer than taking a leap into the unknown? Wouldn't you like to live a richer, happier, more fulfilling life?

As you will see when you read this book, I, too, have experienced painful life challenges. I understand what it is like to have a serious health challenge, a devastating job experience, and dreams that are left to fade.

I faced enormous struggles with low self-confidence and allowed others' opinions to negate my value. And in my desire to find a soul mate, I kissed a lot of frogs as I searched for my prince.

Through it all, I was inspired by spiritual leaders and professional speakers. Most importantly, I listened to the powerful voice inside of me that said, "You deserve the best. Miracles happen."

From reading this book, you will learn how to:

- Make your dreams come true by following eight simple steps

- Communicate effectively so people will help you achieve your goals and dreams

- Handle change in challenging times in order to move forward with ease and confidence

- Value your authentic, unique self

- Overcome barriers to achieving your dreams

- Reframe negative situations so you reach a higher level of success and fulfillment

- Manifest your dreams by asking for what you want

- Value the results of your efforts even when the dream changes

As a motivational speaker, corporate trainer, professor, and professional development coach, I have been teaching these practical skills to thousands of people for more than twenty years. Still, I am continuing to learn and grow just like you.

I would love to hear about your challenges and success as you work toward achieving your goals and dreams. After you finish reading Put Your Dreams to Work, please feel free to let me know about your experiences and how this book has influenced your life.

If you apply the wisdom, skills, and strategies offered in this book, your dreams can and will come true.

With warmest Aloha,

Annabel Chotzen

Honolulu, Hawaii
annabel@annabelchotzen.com
www.annabelchotzen.com

- Chapter 1 -

Opening the Gates

Life is full of challenges. When I think of someone who had a difficult time, I think of Walter. When he was a little boy, Walter lived in Germany. He had a dream of going to America and told his mother and father, "Someday I will live in America."

Walter devoured books by James Fenimore Cooper and other American authors. "America is the land of opportunity, where you can make your dreams come true. That's where I want to live," he would say.

When Walter was twenty, people began to disappear; some were arrested and killed. He had a professor of communications at the university he attended who told him, "Walter, as a Jew, it is very dangerous for you to stay in Germany. If you want to make your dream come true, you must try to escape. And I will help you."

They met secretly and the professor told him, "Walter, when you approach the guard at the border, you must be confident. You cannot show that you have fear. If the guard notices anything is not right, he will arrest you and you could be killed."

Walter responded with anger, "I hate that Nazi guard." The professor said, "Walter, if the guard senses your anger, he will not let you go. Tell me, what do you have in common with that guard?"

Walter thought about it and said, "Well, he is probably about my age. He would likely have a mother and a father like I do, maybe a brother and sister." The more Walter thought about what he might have in common with the guard, the less angry he felt.

The professor said, "Now Walter, let's practice what you will do and say when you meet the guard at the border. Remember, you will have only one chance."

The professor went on, "Walter, how you appear is very important. Your facial expressions are critical. Look the guard in his eyes and smile appropriately. You must appear confident and friendly. Your words should be few, and you must practice what you are going to say.

Make sure that all your papers are in perfect order. And remember always to say thank you." Walter practiced speaking out loud what he would say to the guard, and the professor gave him feedback.

The professor said something very interesting. "Walter, vividly imagine the result that you want. Close your eyes. See yourself speaking easily and confidently with the guard. Imagine the guard gesturing for you to move forward. See the gates opening. This will make all the difference!"

Walter closed his eyes and as instructed, saw himself driving to freedom. Then the professor said, "Walter, it is time. You must go. May God bless you."

If Walter was lucky enough to make it to the other side of the border, he would need to have money to survive, but if the guard knew he had lots of money, it would be obvious that he was trying to escape.

Walter took a small glass vial, filled it with money, and dropped it in a can of oil to conceal it. Walter then hid the can in the trunk of his car and drove to the border.

At the border, a guard yelled, "Halt! Don't move. Show me your papers." Walter was terrified. He felt sweat on his brow and the palms of his hands. His heart was rapidly pounding.

However, Walter had practiced for this moment. He had vividly imagined that he would successfully cross the border and eventually reach the shores of America.

Walter handed his neatly organized papers to the guard. He smiled at the guard, looked squarely in his eyes, and said, "Good day, sir. How are you today?" with a warm voice.

The guard searched the car for any evidence of an attempted escape. If caught, Walter would probably be killed as many of his family and friends had been.

The guard saw the can. He picked it up and shook it. There was a rattling sound inside. The guard looked at Walter. Their eyes met. The seconds felt like hours.

For some unknown reason, the guard put the can back, smiled at Walter, and with a sweeping gesture of his arm said, "Drive on!" The gate swung open and Walter drove to freedom.

Walter soon arrived in America where he met his beloved wife Carla, also a German Jewish refugee. They had eight children. Many years later, Walter celebrated his eighty-fifth birthday in Honolulu, Hawaii. I know because I was there. Walter is my father!

We all have gates we must go through, and often there is a guard at the gate. How we communicate with that gatekeeper can make all the difference. In Walter's case, it was the difference between life and death.

If Walter had not survived, I would not be here today, nor would my seven brothers and sisters, or Walter's fifteen grandchildren, including my son Devin.

Even as a little girl, I recognized how precious life was. I felt so lucky to be alive. I was fascinated by my dad's story of escape; it made me realize that our effectiveness in communicating determines whether or not the gates will open for us and allow us to achieve our dreams, and even whether we live or die.

Walter and Carla taught my siblings and me that life is too precious to waste. "Reach for your dreams," they often said.

As children, my three brothers, four sisters, and I grew up knowing we were deeply loved. We were also given wings to fly with—belief, support, and encouragement to pursue our dreams. "Whatever it is you want, whatever your dream, pursue it now!" our parents told us.

If we don't treat our dreams with urgency, the days, weeks, months, and years go by. We get to the end of our lives feeling disappointed and thinking, "I wish I had done that."

Walter and Carla raised my brothers and sisters and me in Seattle because the beautiful snow-filled mountains where we went skiing reminded them of Germany. However, the winters in Seattle are long, with lots of gray weather and rain.

One day, Walter said, "Let's take a trip to Hawaii." We arrived in Hawaii and camped on several islands. We slept in the pineapple fields on Lanai and on the beaches of Kauai.

One day after a beautiful ocean swim, my father said to me, "Annabelli (that is what he called me), I have a dream of living in Hawaii."

I had seen so many elderly tourists who could barely walk and seemed to have finally made it to Hawaii for a brief visit. I did not want my dad to wait until he was feeble or it was too late. I said, "Dad, do it now!"

A couple of months later, after selling his business in Seattle, Walter moved our family to Hawaii. My mother told me how grateful she was that I had urged my father to move as soon as possible and not wait. We were thrilled to live in this beautiful paradise.

Even now, years later, I give thanks each morning when I awake to the melodious sounds of multi-colored birds as they excitedly welcome a new day.

I swim in the ocean several times a week, caressed and reenergized by the silky, soft ocean waves. The ocean always resets my whole being to a healthy, happy state.

One afternoon, my father and I were sitting on the peak of Olomana Mountain, overlooking Kailua Beach, when he said, "Annabelli, I have another dream."

I said, "Dad, what could it possibly be? You have a beautiful family (of course, I was complimenting myself), you live in one of the most beautiful places in the world, what could you possibly want?"

He said, "I want to be an actor." I replied, "Then you should take acting classes." He said, "There isn't time; the audition is tomorrow."

The next day, Walter auditioned for *Magnum P.I.* and he got the part of Ice Pick, the Mafia guy—the mean and nasty old man who sweats in the sauna with a white towel wrapped around his waist in the episode "Past Tense." That's my dad. And there he was, on national television!

From Walter, I learned eight steps to achieving any dream:

Step 1. Know Your Dream

The first step toward manifesting a dream is to know what it is. Many people have dreams but have buried them inside themselves, believing they really can't have what they want.

"I am too young, too old, not educated enough, have too much to do, don't have time, am not worth it, do not want to disrupt the status quo, don't have enough money, am surrounded by people who don't believe in achieving their dreams," etc.

What is your dream? Do you want to fly around the world and visit many countries? Do you want to meet your soul mate and get married? Do you want to fly an airplane, write a best-selling book, have children, own a business, or own a beautiful home?

Step 2. Vividly Imagine What You Want

The second step is to imagine vividly what it is you want as if it is actually happening. Close your eyes, relax, breathe deeply, and then see yourself achieving your dream. Be as specific and detailed as possible. What does your dream look like? How will it feel when your dream comes true?

Step 3. Have a Sense of Urgency

With urgency, you move much more quickly toward achieving what it is you really want. You don't put things off and say, "I can do that later, tomorrow, another time." Urgency accelerates the process of making your dreams come true.

How much do you want your dream to come true? What will happen if you don't achieve it? If you don't feel urgent about accomplishing your dreams, the days, weeks, months, and years will go by and you won't do what it takes to reach them.

You will come to the end of your life and say, "I wish I had done that." Decide that now is the time you will take action to make your dream a reality. It's up to you to make it a greater priority than it has been up to this point in your life.

Step 4. Make a Plan

You must have a plan. Write down your plan and be as detailed as possible about when, where, and what you will do to achieve your dream. Prioritize the steps necessary to achieve your dream.

Be realistic about how much time you expect it to take to reach each goal. Create a timeline and add or update it as needed. People who make a plan and follow it achieve dreams much more quickly than those who just talk about it.

Step 5. Take Action

Now that you have a plan, it's time to take action. What will you do today and this week to achieve your dreams? Make a commitment to follow your plan! Now is the time to "just do it"!

Step 6. Persevere

Making a dream come true will not always be easy, but you must be willing to do whatever it takes. Like the kukui nuts in Hawaii, which have rough ridges on them, the pathway to your dreams may not be smooth.

It may be difficult, but you need to keep going even during the tough times when things seem impossible. As you pursue your goal, you must persevere. Don't give up!

Step 7. Continually Focus on Your Dreams

We all get sidetracked by the day-to-day details of our busy lives. Often, we forget that we even have dreams.

You must write your dream down and put it where you will see it—on the refrigerator, on the mirror, in your car, next to your computer—so that you are reminded to focus on it every day.

A dream is like a best friend—both will fade away if you fail to cherish them and give them the attention they deserve.

Step 8. Allow a Higher Power to Help You

There is guidance and assistance available to you in a non-physical form. Many people refer to this energy as God. Native Americans call it the Great Spirit. There are many names. Whatever you believe your Higher Power to be, ask for help to make your dream come true.

The focus of my work has been to empower people to achieve all they desire in life. To make your dreams come true, you need the support of other people. You must have harmony, instead of conflict.

You need skills to get along well with all types of people so they will open the gates for you. Then you can move forward and achieve your goals and dreams. My goal with this book is to help you do exactly that.

Questions for Reflection

1. What is it that you really want? What are your dreams?

2. What is your plan to make your dreams come true?

3. What actions do you need to take?

4. How can you make your dreams urgent?

- Chapter 2 -

Handling Change in Challenging Times

Being able to adjust to change in our lives is critically important in order to achieve our dreams. When we go through a crisis, a health challenge, a death, a loss of a job, a divorce—it can feel terrifying, unbearable, and overwhelming. It is like standing at Kilauea Volcano when suddenly it erupts, wildly spewing lava.

I was there once when the volcano erupted. It happened when I was visiting Kilauea Volcano with my mother and father and we decided to hike around the lava fields. Little did we know that we were in a danger zone.

A river of molten lava was a foot away from where we were walking. I stood next to the life-threatening river of hot lava, knowing that I could instantly die if it came any closer. It was frightening. As soon as we overcame our shock, we quickly ran to safety!

When you experience a crisis in your life, you may feel as if you are going to die. You think it is too difficult to live without the loved one, with the health challenge, with the loss. You feel upset, fearful, or grief-stricken.

After a while, you get accustomed to the loss and life continues. You are still angry and upset, but you adjust to living with the change that has occurred.

This situation is like the red hot lava. After erupting from the volcano, it begins to slow down as it moves toward the sea. Slowly, the lava becomes hard, cold, dry, and lifeless, allowing nothing to grow on it. Without realizing it, people stop focusing on their dreams and become trapped in the hardened lava.

I have a friend whose husband left her thirty years ago. She never dated again. She still says to me, "If only my husband hadn't left, my life would be perfect." She is stuck in her own lava field.

I have another friend who was married for twenty years. One day, his wife said to him, "I'm tired of you, and I'm tired of living in Hawaii. I'm moving to Michigan." The man was devastated.

He went to a counselor who told him, "I want you to write down twenty things that are good about this." The man said, "There is nothing good about this. I'm heartbroken!"

The counselor told him to think of things that could be good about the separation. My friend wrote: "I now have more time to devote to my new business. I volunteer to help other people. I can spend time with friends. Maybe someday I will meet a woman who loves me even more than my wife did...." He created a list of twenty items.

The counselor told him, "Imagine what you want in your life, as if it is happening, and you will begin to believe it can be your reality." Every morning, and before he went to bed at night, my friend would close his eyes and imagine what his life would be like if he had everything he wanted.

He saw himself having meaningful work that helped humanity, a loving wife, supportive friends, good health, and strong spirituality.

One day, after vividly imagining his perfect life for several weeks, he met a wonderful woman. They got married. Though he never thought he would be a father, they had a beautiful baby boy. This man is my husband, Will!

When you are going through a crisis in your life, remember to focus continually on what it is that you want—your life vision. Instead of fearing change, embrace change. The Hawaiian word for change is *ho'ololi*. It is a very important word with deep meaning.

I often ask the people in my audiences to say *ho'ololi* several times as they stand and stretch their arms to the sky. When you welcome change, you can see all that is good about a situation. You become grateful and can more easily imagine your life just the way you want it to be.

Whatever you focus on will multiply. If you focus on negativity, anger, and grief, that will increase. If you are optimistic and imagine a wonderful life, good things are likely to come to you more quickly.

Have the courage to change your mind, to see things differently, to take a different view, and to try new things. Sometimes the loss of one dream leads to the creation of a greater dream.

When you focus on what's good about the situation, have gratitude for everything in your life, and vividly imagine what you want, it is as if you have planted seeds underneath the hard, cold, dry lava.

Miraculously, the seeds begin to sprout and push their way through the lava. Lush plants grow and flowers blossom. Soon your life will become a paradise.

Like the seeds sprouting, growing, and pushing through the lava, you too can leave your dark situation. Believe in yourself. Reach for the light of a new, wonderful life.

Although my husband was devastated when his first wife left him, he ended up finding happiness with me and our beautiful son, Devin.

Next time you feel distraught, ask what's good about this situation. Write it down. Count your blessings, and name them one by one. Watch your good unfold!

Questions for Reflection

1. Are you resisting or embracing change?

2. When times are difficult, do you stay focused on your dreams?

3. What do you need to focus on to make your life a true paradise?

4. Do you take time to vividly imagine all you want as if it is happening now?

5. If you are experiencing difficulty or a change, make a list of the positive outcomes caused by it.

- Chapter 3 -

The Platinum Rule

In order to open the gates to your dreams, you must have the cooperation of the people who are gatekeepers. How you communicate with them will make all the difference as to whether you have great success or defeat and failure.

Just as Walter practiced his new communication skills before meeting the guard, you must have outstanding communication skills so that the gates will open for you to achieve your dreams. Chapters 3 to 7 discuss these important aspects of communication.

We need skills to get along well with all types of people so they will open the gates for us. We must have harmony instead of conflict. Then we can move forward and achieve our goals and dreams.

If Walter had not had a positive interaction with the guard, I would not be here today, nor would my seven brothers and sisters and Walter's fifteen grandchildren. From the time I was a little girl, I knew how lucky I was to be alive. I also realized that how well we communicate with one another is critical to whether we have success or failure in life, or even whether we survive, as in Walter's case.

How do we get other people to open the gates for us? As a child, I learned about the Golden Rule: "Do unto others as you would have them do unto you." Since this was the Golden Rule, I assumed it was the best rule to follow to get along well with other people.

After all, the Golden Rule is about being kind, caring, and thoughtful toward others. I decided early in life that if I followed this rule, I would have peace and harmony with everyone and life would be smooth sailing.

Often, it didn't happen that way. I noticed that people everywhere were having a lot of conflict, even though they usually had good intentions and were claiming to follow the Golden Rule.

Most people are doing unto others the way they would want to be done unto. The problem is many people do not always like the way they are being done unto.

The way you want to be treated may differ from how others want to be treated. And when people feel mistreated, they become angry and disillusioned. The success of the family or work team then suffers.

When I first got married, on a special occasion, like my husband's birthday, I would give him flowers because I love flowers. One day, he said, "Sweetheart, thanks for the flowers, but they really don't do that much for me."

I asked him, "What do you want?" He said, "A shirt." I bought him a bright red shirt—because I love red. I found out quickly that he didn't like red; he liked blue. I had practiced the Golden Rule when buying gifts for him, but it hadn't worked out the way I intended.

There is a better rule for getting along with other people. It's called the Platinum Rule: "Do unto others the way they want to be done unto."

The trick is to figure out what other people want and then give it to them. Of course you should maintain your own integrity and feel good about the interaction. I wish I had learned this rule forty years ago because it would have made my life less stressful and more productive.

Knowing that one of the greatest difficulties people have is getting along with other people, I decided to embark on a lifelong journey. I chose to spend my life solving the mystery of how to get along with all kinds of people regardless of their background so that there would be peace and joy in my life and peace on earth.

Whether someone is your boss, a spouse, or a child, when you fill another person's needs, you can have outstanding relationships. People with whom you have great relationships will open the gates for you. You then can walk through those gates and achieve your goals and dreams.

Questions for Reflection

1. Do you follow the Golden Rule?

2. Can you also follow the Platinum Rule?

3. How good are you at giving other people what they want and need?

4. How well do you get along with everyone in your life?

Chapter 4

Listening to Other People

One of people's greatest needs is to be listened to and understood. That doesn't mean you have to agree with them, but they must know you understand their viewpoints.

Most people are not very good listeners. Have you ever found yourself talking about something that is really important to you, and when you pause for a second, the other person interrupts and says, "Well, what happened to me was..."?

How did that make you feel? Not very good. People are often cut off in the middle of their thoughts or sentences.

Do you want more clients or customers for your business? Do you want to have wonderful friends? One of the keys to successful business and personal relationships is being a good listener. In my workshops, participants practice becoming great listeners. Here are five important steps to becoming a great listener:

1. Show Interest in the Other Person. When you are listening, look into the person's eyes, nod to show you are listening, and smile. When the person pauses, do not interrupt.

Many people are uncomfortable with silence, so they jump in to fill the void when the other person stops talking. That makes the person feel like you don't really care about them or what they are saying. When you interrupt, it tells the other person that you care more about yourself.

What should you do if you don't know whether they are finished or not? Smile and breathe. Take time. Make sure the person has completed their entire thought. If you are on the phone, say "Ah "or "Yes" to let the person know you are listening.

2. Echo What the Person Has Said. When you are certain the person has completed their thought, repeat back some of the words you heard. Use their same words. This makes the person feel listened to and understood.

When we paraphrase what we think the other person said and use different words, it may not be what the person intended. This can cause the person to feel irritated and angry.

They may even tell you, "That is not what I said." When we repeat back what the other person said it makes them feel listened to and understood.

3. Ask Open-Ended Questions. When we ask people questions, it shows that we are interested in them, and this makes them feel cared about. "What did you think about that? How did that make you feel? What do you need?"

Most people do not ask other people questions but asking people questions makes them feel you genuinely care about who they are and are interested in what they think and feel.

In addition, if you ask people questions and then really listen to their answers, you will get a clear picture of what they need.

I ask people so many questions and come home with so much information that my husband thinks I should have been a detective!

At training sessions, people have said to me, "I would have given that person what they wanted, if I had known. But I didn't know what they wanted until it was too late."

I reply, "Did you ask them questions? Did you ask them what they wanted and needed?" The person will often say something like, "I did not ask questions because I did not want to intrude.... I did not want to seem too forward.... I am too shy." There are always excuses.

If you don't ask questions, you will have a much more difficult time getting the answers you are looking for. Often, people won't volunteer information. They will be thinking, "I can take my business elsewhere. I can find someone else to help me."

Make sure you ask people questions and then really listen to their answers without interrupting. This will save you a lot of time because you will get it right the first time.

4. Summarize What You Heard the Person Say. In order to be certain about what the person wants or needs, take note of the key points you heard and write them down. This process will help you remember what was said and what you heard.

Then reiterate the points you heard to make sure you clearly understood what the person said. Say, "If I understand you, what you are feeling is…. What you want is…. What you need is…." The other person can then fill in any missing information.

5. Confirm. I used to think I should not waste another person's time, so when I thought the purpose of the meeting was accomplished, I would be the one to say, "Thank you very much." Then I would get up to leave or end the phone conversation.

Instead, I have learned to ask whether there is anything else the person needs or wants to talk about. This final step is very important because it is the point in business where people may say, "Actually, I do need something else."

Often, I can give the person the additional things they need, or I can recommend someone else who can help them. It is a win-win situation.

Questions for Reflection

1. Are you a good listener?

2. Do you ask people questions about themselves and their work?

3. Are you able to remain silent without interrupting?

Chapter 5

Understanding Different People

Wouldn't it be great if when you meet someone, you could instantly read their mind? You would know what was important to the person, how they liked to receive information, and what it would take to get along with them.

Unfortunately, most of us aren't mind readers. The next best thing is to understand that people have different personalities.

When we understand and communicate effectively with different personality types, we can get along with other people, work well together in teams, and move forward in very positive ways at work and at home.

Here are five personality types I created that will help you understand how people are different. I named each type to describe the essence of that personality.

1. Analyzers are the hardest workers. They are very detail-oriented and meticulous. They like data, facts, and numbers, and they are logical and practical.

Analyzers prefer to work alone because each one of them believes they are the best person to get the job done. They do not like distractions and appreciate or even insist on focused discussions.

2. Bottom Liners are ambitious and decisive. They want you to get to the point! When they want something, they want it right now and expect people to get the job done without a lot of interaction or discussion. They are focused on the bottom line and achieving the goal.

Bottom Liners are willing to make tough decisions and are not concerned about how other people are feeling. They know they are right, and they are rarely willing to admit they are wrong. They must always win.

3. Expanders are detail-oriented like Analyzers, but they want to stretch and grow, try new things, and get out of their boxes. They are searching and growing and in a constant state of transition. Expanders are courageous. They like to be given new challenges and are excited about change.

4. People Persons care most about relationships and helping other people. They have a lot of empathy for people, can talk to anyone, and really want to make a positive impact on people's lives.

They are the best communicators, best listeners, and are genuinely interested in other people. They are also concerned about what others think about them.

5. Conceptualizers are visionaries who are dramatic, intuitive, and full of creative ideas. They are excellent at thinking outside the box.

Conceptualizers like to juggle many different activities at the same time and get bored working on only one project. They prefer working on the big picture and are not good with details.

Getting Along with Different Personality Types

Analyzers: In order to get along with an Analyzer, you must do your homework and be prepared. Put information in writing with facts, figures, and as many details as possible.

Do not rush Analyzers. They need to have plenty of time and like to be left alone while they are in the decision-making process. Analyzers do not change quickly and need to consider all the ramifications of a decision before moving forward.

Bottom Liners: The way to get along with a Bottom Liner is to be logical and not emotional. Get to the point and don't beat around the bush. Allow the bottom liner to be right. Wait until they are in a good mood before you meet with them.

Never disagree or argue with a Bottom Liner because you will lose. Always find a way to let them think they have won.

Expanders: In order to get along with an Expander, suggest new, interesting, and challenging things to do. Ask the

Expander what they would like to do rather than just telling them. Always look for a win-win solution. Give in on unimportant matters.

People Persons: The most important way to get along with the People Person is to show that you care about them and other people. People Persons can often change their minds, so be flexible and cooperative.

Do not push them around. Be sure to maintain your emotional control because People Persons can be very emotional. Always assure confidentiality and privacy.

Conceptualizers: The best way to get along with a Conceptualizer is to listen to their creative ideas with an open mind. Allow the Conceptualizer to completely express everything they need to.

If they get sidetracked, steer the conversation back to the main topic. It is difficult for Conceptualizers to focus on details. They are more interested in the big picture.

Understanding the Dynamics Between Personality Types

The Analyzer does not need to be right like the Bottom Liner, but they get along well because they are both focused on facts and details. The Analyzer doesn't mind the Bottom Liner being right as long as the information is correct.

Bottom Liners have difficulty getting along with other Bottom Liners because they both need to be right. Imagine putting your hands in fists and then knocking your fists together. This is what happens when you put two Bottom Liners together who have different positions.

Analyzers get along well with People Persons. People Persons are very sociable and emotional, but they need the back-up, detail-oriented solidity that is offered by Analyzers. Analyzers are more likely to keep to themselves, but they find balance with the People Persons.

Analyzers have a lot of difficulty getting along with Conceptualizers. The Analyzer looks at a Conceptualizer and says, "How can you live that way? You are so disorganized!"

The Conceptualizer looks at the Analyzer and says, "How can you live that way? You are so structured and boring!"

It is difficult for Bottom Liners and People Persons to get along. The Bottom Liner has to be right and doesn't care how other people feel. The People Person doesn't care about anything else unless everyone is happy.

Expanders get along with all the personality types. They are detail-oriented so they are compatible with Analyzers and Bottom Liners. They don't have to be right and are open minded. They also look outward to expand and grow so they enjoy People Persons and Conceptualizers.

Since Conceptualizers are mainly concerned with the big picture and ideas, they have a hard time getting along with the fact- and detail-oriented Analyzers and Bottom Liners.

When Conceptualizers are able to give some specifics to their thoughts, they will be able to communicate better with Analyzers and Expanders.

If you are in a position of authority, determine the end result; then assign the right personality for the job. To prevent conflict, match the personality type to the task and assign complementary personalities to work together.

Although we each have one dominant personality type, most people are a combination of different personality types. For example, I am predominantly a People Person, but when I am in a leadership position, I am more like an Analyzer since I am required to deal with budgets, facts, and figures.

When you identify a person's predominant personality type and approach that person based on who they are rather than on who you are, conflict and disharmony can be avoided.

You are then more likely to get along well with all types of people because you are practicing the Platinum Rule: treat other people the way they want to be treated. When you easily get along with all kinds of people, the doors to achieving your dreams and goals are more likely to open.

Questions for Reflection

1. What is your predominant personality type?

2. Whom have you had conflict with, and what is that person's personality type?

3. Can you list three things you can do to have a better relationship with that person?

Chapter 6

Resolving Conflict

Even though we hone our listening skills, chances are conflicts may still arise. We may have nothing to do with the origin of the conflict, but the more we know how to minimize conflict with other people, the faster we can achieve our goals and dreams.

If we have conflict with someone, that person won't want to help us. In order to achieve our dreams, we must have the tools to resolve conflict quickly.

Defusing Upset People

It is very important to know how to defuse upset people. When someone is upset, we must know how to help them calm down. Otherwise, like a string of firecrackers once lit, the person may quickly explode.

The first thing you need to do is have the person sit down. I have never seen someone fighting who is seated, have you? Once people are seated, they automatically feel more relaxed.

A great way to defuse upset people is to acknowledge their point of view. If the person is right, you can say, "You are right; you are absolutely right. I agree with you."

People like it if you say you agree with them. It helps them feel better. I am rarely upset, but once in a while if I am, my husband will say, "I agree with you," and that immediately calms me down. Then I tell him, "That isn't fair; you attended my workshops."

If you are not sure whether the other person is right, you can still give acknowledgment by saying, "You may be right," or "It is possible that…" or "Let me check further."

If you tell someone that you will get back to them, give them a day and time when you will respond and put it on your calendar. It is a commitment.

Even if you don't have the answer, you need to let them know you are still working on solving their problem. If you forget to call back, it will make the person even angrier and further damage the relationship.

If the person has done something wrong, yet is very angry and upset, you can still give them empathy, remembering that no one is perfect and we have all made mistakes.

You can say, "I appreciate how you are feeling.… I am sorry that happened.… I know how hard this must be for you." And then listen without interrupting or giving advice unless they ask for it.

In our Western culture, when people have done something wrong, they are frequently abandoned by friends, family, and coworkers. If we are there for a person when times are tough, they will often feel tremendous gratitude and may be there for us in return during difficult times.

I do believe that the good we give to others comes back to us. When we open the gates for others, we help them achieve their dreams.

To Resolve Conflict, Focus on Common Interests, Not Positions

One of the most important ways to resolve conflict is to focus on common interests rather than getting stuck on your own personal positions.

When we are completely focused on our positions, such as "I am a Democrat" or "I am a Republican," and we try to solve a problem with a person of another position, it doesn't work.

Often, things get worse and the result is a stalemate. Nothing gets resolved. We see this in our nation's capital where there is so much fighting and disagreement between the two parties that very little gets accomplished. It is very disillusioning.

To help people understand the difference between conflict and cooperation, I ask workshop participants to close their fists. I tell them that each fist represents a position. Then

I tell them to knock their fists together. I ask them how it feels.

They reply that it feels uncomfortable or it hurts. Then I ask the participants to open their hands and intertwine the fingers of one hand with the other. I ask them how this feels and they reply that it feels good.

When we focus on our common interests such as health, safety, family, and security, it is like intertwining our fingers. We can come together, feel good about one another, and solve problems.

Whenever you have a conflict with a person, whether at work or at home, focus on what you both have in common instead of your different positions. By focusing on your common interests, you build rapport with that person, which makes you much more likely to resolve the conflict.

Do you notice how friends find ways of resolving problems? The reason is the relationship is more important than who wins or loses. There is a strong desire to bring happiness to the other person and protect the friendship. We care more about the other person than we do about being right.

While working on controversial projects in the public and private sectors, I learned a great deal about how to resolve conflict.

In one project, the mayor of the city wanted to place low-income families in upper-income neighborhoods because studies have shown that people tend to emulate the people around them. He felt it would encourage the low-income families to strive for higher goals, thus breaking the cycle of poverty.

The mayor said, "Annabel, I want you to take a leadership role in this program and have meetings in the neighborhoods where we plan to place low-income families. Make a presentation about our plans, listen to community comments, and propose solutions. Will you do it?" I said, "Of course" because I couldn't refuse the mayor.

And then, just to add a little more pressure, he said, "This program must be a success. I am counting on being reelected in two years."

I felt the enormity of his request, but I also relished the idea of meeting with nice people in friendly neighborhoods. Little did I realize the amount of anger and hostility that would greet me at every community meeting.

While initially a lot of enthusiastic support existed in the community for this program, when middle income and well to do people found out that poor families would be moving into their neighborhoods, their attitudes changed from amiable to hostile.

Large crowds attended the meetings. The boisterous upper-income people held protest signs and yelled, "We don't want this program in our neighborhood!"

One man was especially loud and vociferous. His name was Tony, and he was very wealthy. He attended every meeting regardless of where it was held. Tony was a large man with a booming voice, and he was vehemently opposed to this program.

One day, I invited Tony out for lunch. For two hours, Tony talked. During that time, I resisted the temptation to share my views or try to persuade him about the program's benefits.

I just listened. I don't think many people listened to Tony because he talked and talked as if no one had ever listened to him before.

He spoke about his childhood. He said, "Annabel, when I was a boy, my family was very poor. Often, I would go to sleep hungry because we ran out of food before my mother could get food stamps again.

Throughout the night, I listened to my stomach growling. I had holes in my clothes and my feet hurt because my shoes were too small.

The worst part was that the kids would stand outside of our house, point and laugh because our house was falling apart. I don't want to be reminded of how terrible it felt to be poor. I don't want those families moving into my neighborhood."

Suddenly Tony paused, tears streamed down his cheeks and it was several moments before he could control himself sufficiently to speak. He was sharing and releasing something very painful—something that had been buried deep inside him for a long time.

After having several lunches together, Tony and I became good friends. I never tried to push the merits of the housing program. We shared many things we had in common, like coming from large families and the struggles our families had experienced.

One day, Tony said, "We should have background checks on all the families. This would quell the concerns of the people who live in these neighborhoods." And then he said, "Why don't we give this neighborhood a park?

Many families will be moving in, and they could use a park. That would make the rest of the neighbors very happy too."

He went on to say, "Why don't we put a beautiful statue or mural in this neighborhood?" Tony got very excited as he came up with many good ideas and ways of addressing people's concerns.

Before long, Tony became the leader of the housing program. By the time I was ready to leave Seattle to go to graduate school, low-income families had moved into those neighborhoods.

The last time I saw Tony, he gave me a huge bear hug. I felt sad to say goodbye. Tony said, "Annabel, we did it!" The program was a success and the mayor got reelected.

I learned from Tony that when we focus on common interests rather than getting stuck on positions, we can solve problems and move forward.

I also learned that listening instead of talking is critical to understanding people's concerns. When we really listen to others, we often realize that the real reason they are upset is not always immediately evident.

One of the important components of making our dreams come true is being able to resolve conflict with other people. When there is discord in relationships, it holds us back from achieving our goals. We always need to focus on our similarities rather than our differences.

Be Open to Unusual Ways of Resolving Conflict

My parents desired to leave the rainy weather in Seattle and move to a warmer climate. They were thinking about Mexico, Hawaii, or Israel. They decided to send me to Israel as their "investigative delegate" to check out our Jewish heritage.

I think they were anxious to get me launched and kick me out of the nest, as far away as possible. After high school, I went to Israel for a year.

When my sister Vonny came to visit me, we decided to hike to the monastery at the top of Mt. Tabor. Cars drove up a long, winding road, but we decided to take a shortcut through the woods.

Shortly after we entered the thick forest, a large man suddenly jumped out of the bushes! He had huge brown muscles glistening with sweat. His dark, slightly crossed eyes were intently focused on me. Pointing a sharp stick, he said in Arabic, "I want you!" and lunged toward me.

I was filled with terror. I looked for a stick or a rock, something to protect myself with. I thought we would have to fight. I imagined horrible things that would happen to my sister and me. I considered making a run for it as fast as I could. I saw no alternatives.

Then Vonny said, "Annabel, put your arm around him." I said, "Are you crazy?" Her voice was firm and in control, so I did what she told me to do. I put my arm around him on one side, and she put her arm around him on the other side. "Hold him tightly," she said.

We began to hike very fast up the mountain, holding this man between us. Now and then, he would begin to pull away, each time saying he wanted to kiss me.

Vonny told him to kiss her instead. We kept climbing, going as fast as we could up the mountain, tightly held in a three-way embrace. I have never hiked so fast! We were sweating profusely.

Finally, we reached the top. We saw the monastery in the distance surrounded by a moat.

When the man saw the monastery, a look of fear appeared on his face. Then he suddenly leaped into the bushes and disappeared as suddenly as he had appeared at the bottom of the mountain. We were safe! Out of breath, but safe!

I was totally in awe of my sister. The way she had reacted to this tense situation saved our lives. She responded with loving kindness instead of reacting with fear. Later, she told me she had only been thinking about survival.

I learned an important lesson: When we have conflict with other people, we must challenge ourselves to think of creative solutions that bring people together, rather than destroy our existence. Our survival depends on it!

Questions for Reflection

1. How good are you at defusing upset people?

2. How can you improve your conflict resolution skills?

3. What are some unusual, creative things you have done to resolve conflict?

Chapter 7

Communication Effectiveness

It has been said that when our message is received by others, only 7 percent is conveyed by the words, 38 percent by the sound of our voice, and 55 percent by our body language.

To be effective at communicating, we need to practice and be aware not only of our choice of words, but the sound of our voice and how our body language appears to others.

If I say to my son, "I love you" with no vocal warmth, it does not sound believable. If I use a warm vocal inflection and also give him a hug, my message is far more likely to be received.

In one of my leadership development workshops, there was a doctor who looked very angry. She was frowning and never smiled.

She told the group that her kids and husband think she is mad when she is not, and patients who see her in the hospital think she is angry. If people had not told her how she appeared, she would not have been aware of it.

I suggested she put a large mirror in her office so she could see her expressions. She laughed at this idea, but when she did, she had the most gorgeous smile. I told her how beautiful she looked when she smiled.

She did place a mirror in her office and became so surprised to see her expressions. She practiced smiling and now has a new habit of smiling and making all those around her feel good!

I am a very happy person and love to smile. My husband tends to be serious, yet he has a great sense of humor. Sometimes when he looks very serious, I will stand in front of him and smile, and then suggest that he smile too. He puts on a fake smile and then laughs.

I also suggest to people that if they have trouble sleeping at night, they smile as they go to sleep. Smiling makes us happier so that we can relax, be peaceful, and sleep well.

Questions for Reflection

1. How does your body language appear to other people?

2. Do you smile and make eye contact?

3. What does your voice sound like?

4. Does the tone and inflection of your voice match your words and facial expressions?

Giving Appreciations

People tend to focus on the negative things about others that irritate them. Just as we must have gratitude in our lives for all the good things we have, we need to focus on what other people are doing well!

One of the most important things anyone can do to improve a relationship is to "give appreciations." This means saying words of appreciation for what another person did or just for who they are. Just a few simple words can make all the difference in how someone feels.

Giving appreciations is a key to a happy marriage and good relationships with our children, bosses, and employees. When we appreciate another person, not only does that person feel good, but we also begin focusing on that person in a positive light.

Suddenly, we notice all the good things they are doing and we are delighted to have them in our life. Whatever we focus on multiplies!

When you are giving appreciations to another person, be as specific as possible. For example, say:

- I appreciate it when you….

- I really like it when you….

- I like the way you….

- It meant a lot to me when you....

- Thank you for....

- You did a good job....

There may be times when conflicts arise and you need to confront the other person. If you have been giving sincere appreciations to your colleagues or family members on a regular basis, you will have made a lot of deposits into their emotional bank accounts and developed a sense of trust with them. A small withdrawal, such as a suggestion for improvement, will not hurt those relationships.

In the event that you want to bring about positive change in someone else's behavior, I recommend the sandwich approach. It is an effective way of communicating something that may be difficult for the other person to hear.

First, say something you appreciate about the person, being as specific as possible. Next, tactfully make your suggestion for improvement. Finally, end on a positive note of appreciation for that person. This sandwiches the negative between the two positives.

For example, if someone is always arriving late to work, you can say, "We value your contribution to this company. When you are late, it seems like you don't respect the team.

COMMUNICATION EFFECTIVENESS

We expect everyone to arrive on time. We want you to remedy this because everyone appreciates your excellent skills and enjoys working with you."

I find that when someone gives me a suggestion for improvement, if it is sandwiched between appreciations, I am able to accept it much more easily. Try this approach next time.

Other ways of appreciating people include giving gifts, sending beautiful handwritten cards, or taking them out to lunch. My neighbors leave fragrant flowers, papayas, and avocados at our door in the morning. Imagine waking up to such beautiful gifts. It just makes our day!

And of course, we give right back to them. By joyfully giving and receiving, our lives become rich and abundant.

Questions for Reflection

1. How do you show appreciation to other people for all the things they do?

2. Is there someone you should show appreciation to? Do it now!

3. In what situation can you use the sandwich approach to effect a change in someone?

- Chapter 8 -

The Power to Manifest Your Dreams

One day, several years ago, I was sitting under a kukui tree with my Hawaiian friend, Kalani. He was just getting his PhD in Philosophy, so we were enjoying talking about the meaning of life.

He picked up a kukui nut, rolled the rough ridge-like nut between his fingers, and then held it up. Emphatically, he said, "Hold this nut, carry it with you, focus on your dream, and your dream will come true."

I said, "Kalani, what do you mean?" He said, "My wise Hawaiian grandmother taught me about the many uses of the kukui nut. The oil was used for light before Hawaiians had electricity.

The oil is also used to heal burns and to improve digestion. My grandmother taught me that if you carry the kukui nut with you and focus on your dream, your dream will come true."

The kukui nut comes from the kukui tree, the Hawaii state tree. Kukui means light or enlightenment. As we looked up at the tree, we noticed that the leaves of the kukui tree are dull on one side and shiny on the other. When you see a hillside of kukui trees, leaves shimmering in the sunshine, it looks like the whole hillside is glowing.

I wanted to see whether Kalani's advice would work, so at my workshops I gave each member of my audience a kukui nut; then I instructed them to close their eyes and focus on their dreams.

I led them through a guided meditation. I told them to feel the light of the kukui nut bringing light and enlightenment to their dreams.

Now, I include this deep and powerful Kukui Nut Celebration at the end of my "Put Your Dreams to Work" presentation, one of my most popular workshops.

I have received the most amazing testimonies from people who carried their kukui nut with them and focused on their dream. One mother told me that every day her young son, who was having difficulty with his classes, carried his kukui nut in his pocket as he walked to school. His grades suddenly improved and today he is an "A" student!

Another man said that his wife, who was quite ill at the time, held the kukui nut each day and focused on her dream of getting healthy. She became well in a short amount of time and had peace of mind.

A young student of mine who carried his kukui nut wrote that he kept focusing on his dream of finding the perfect job, and he did. Another person focused on peace and harmony with his coworker, and now they are successful business partners.

One man was tired of working for a large company and assisting the CEO. He wanted to make a difference in the world. Today, this man is the president of his own successful company. He travels the world and says, "I am doing good things for humanity and doing well." He takes his kukui nut with him throughout the world.

The power of belief is amazing. When you focus on what you want and imbue your dream with the light of the kukui nut, it is remarkable how your dreams can easily come true.

As for me, while I carried my kukui nut, I dreamt of meeting a wonderful man, marrying him, and having a beautiful baby. One day, I was sitting with Kalani in Kapiolani Park below Diamond Head. We had just played a set of tennis. Tears welled up and I began to cry.

Kalani said, "Annabel, are you sad because I beat you in tennis?" I said, "No," and then I told him how remarkable it was that for years I had been speaking about making dreams come true and had given thousands of kukui nuts to my audiences.

I was thrilled to hear that many of their dreams were coming true, yet I was sad that my dream of having my own family had not come true. My biological clock was ticking loudly, the alarm ready to go off at any moment.

"Kalani, I can't talk about making dreams come true if I can't realize my own dreams. I'm going to stop speaking until my own dreams have come true," I said sadly.

"Annabel," Kalani replied, "if I were you, I would tell everyone about your dream. In the Hawaiian culture, we openly share our dreams. The whole community can help. It takes lots of people supporting you, believing in you, and helping you to make your dreams come true. Tell everyone what you want."

I followed Kalani's advice. I asked everyone, "Do you know a man who would like to get married and have a baby?" I then made a list of the eligible men who were recommended.

One by one, I invited each one out to lunch. As soon as lunch was served, I would blurt out, "Would you consider marrying me and having a baby?"

It shocked them all. Several of the men were divorced with children. One man was thrilled to marry me if I would support him and his five children. Others just didn't want kids. The luncheons were short-lived. Each man left the restaurant quickly, and I never heard from any of them again.

It was December 22, 1999. The coincidence of the full moon, winter solstice, and the changing of the millennia made it the most auspicious day of the decade. It was the biggest and brightest moon in 135 years and it was shining brightly over Koko Head in Hawaii Kai.

That night, a warm breeze and the sweet smell of fresh plumeria filled the air. My mother was holding a holiday party at her home near Hanauma Bay. There was a man there, tall and handsome with deep brown eyes. His name was Will. I boldly gave him my phone number.

Will invited me to join him for a New Year's Eve celebration in Lanikai, at a beautiful home overlooking the Mokoluas. As fireworks exploded, we sat by a huge outdoor fire, talked about our lives, and got to know each other.

A few days later, I asked Will to attend a symphony concert. I had two tickets but no one to go with. I didn't know at the time that the featured music was Dvorak's New World Symphony, one of Will's favorite pieces.

It symbolizes the transition of moving from the dark and difficult world into the new world of light and joy. As we held hands during the concert, I felt that we were falling in love.

We went out for dinner after the concert. I remembered Kalani's advice about asking everyone to help us achieve our dreams. I asked Will whether he would consider marrying me and having a baby. He didn't seem frightened by my assertive question. He said he would think about my question.

About two weeks later, on January 17, my birthday, Will said he would marry me and be willing to have a baby with me. We had a beautiful wedding next to the ocean with Hawaiian music, friends, and family. A short time after that I got pregnant. My dreams had come true!

Or so I thought. I will never forget the call from the doctor. "Annabel, we don't think your baby is healthy. I want you to come in for an ultrasound test."

Will and I went to the hospital the next day. As the technician was moving the ultrasound sensor over my abdomen, she could not see one of my baby's hands because it was closed in a fist. She said she needed to see all the fingers because there was concern about the baby's health.

At that moment, Will put his head close to my tummy, believing the baby could hear and understand him. He said, "Come on, little guy; give me a high-five." Will put his outstretched hand on my stomach, showing a high-five sign.

As we watched the ultrasound screen, we were amazed to see the baby's hands open up wide. We could clearly see all five fingers. The technician said, "I can't believe it."

A moment later, the baby put his hands together in the prayer position. She said, "Oh my goodness. I've never seen anything like this!"

We still weren't certain if we would have a healthy baby. We spent a few days on the North Shore of Oahu, walked on the beach, and prayed that we would be able to handle whatever happened.

As we were driving home, I suddenly noticed a baby's cradle at a house having a yard sale. I yelled, "Stop! We have to get that." We turned around and bought the beautiful wooden cradle. I felt like it was a sign and an affirmation that our baby would be healthy and we would get to use the cradle.

When our baby was born, he was completely fine. The first thing Will said was "He's so beautiful!" We were elated and felt blessed.

We gave him the first name Devin, from the root word meaning divine, and the middle name Makana, which means gift in Hawaiian. He is our heavenly gift! Today, as proud parents, we exalt in all his achievements, in his brilliance and beauty.

I went back to speaking about making dreams come true and delivering the Hawaii Kukui Nut Celebration. It was far more powerful now that my own dreams had come true.

Questions for Reflection

1. What is your biggest dream?

2. How will you feel when that dream comes true?

3. What steps can you take to make your dream a reality?

Chapter 9

The Hawaii Kukui Nut Celebration

Here are the steps to the Kukui Nut Celebration that I conduct in my seminars where each participant receives their own kukui nut—a gift from Hawaii—to take home.

During the celebration, participants renew their goals, dreams, and life vision. The kukui nut then becomes a focal point of belief and commitment. Lives are changed and results are achieved.

At the Kukui Nut Celebration, I ask participants to hold their kukui nut. You can also hold something that is meaningful to you, such as a crystal or a special stone.

Imagine you are in my audience, listening to my voice as I take you through the Kukui Nut Celebration. The eight steps to achieving your dream are:

1. Know Your Dream
2. Vividly Imagine What You Want
3. Have a Sense of Urgency
4. Make a Plan
5. Continually Focus on Your Dream
6. Take Action
7. Persevere
8. Allow a Higher Power to Help You

Now, hold your kukui nut or other object in the palm of your hand and close your eyes. Imagine you are walking on a path toward your dream. Where are you? What does it feel like as you are walking? Are you walking barefoot in the sand along the ocean?

Are you hiking on a mountain trail? Are you strolling through a park? What is the weather like? Is there sunshine on your shoulders? Is it misty? Do you see a rainbow?

Continue to imagine that you are walking toward your dream. You are tired. It is difficult, and you feel like you want to give up, but you keep going. Something inside of you says, "I really want this. I can do this. I can achieve my dream."

You notice that your dream gets closer and looms larger. What are the colors and shapes you see? Look around you. Along your path, you notice people are cheering for you. They are your friends, family, and loved ones who believe in you.

They may be alive or may be people you love who have passed on. They could be teachers from the past, your parents, grandparents, or great-grandparents. They love you and believe in you. All of them are cheering, "You can do it!"

Finally, you reach your dream. Where are you when your dream comes true? Are you walking on a stage, receiving a standing ovation from hundreds of people? Are you celebrating over a candlelight dinner with one other person? See yourself smiling and saying, "I knew my dream would come true."

This is the essence of the Kukui Nut Celebration. However, there is actually a ninth step—share your dreams. The more you share your dreams with other people, the faster your dreams will come true.

By telling people what you want, you are committing yourself to making your dream a reality. When people think of you, they will think about your dream and give you support, ideas, suggestions, and encouragement, just like my Hawaiian friend Kalani taught me.

At this point, I ask the members of my audience to share their dreams with each other. For you, my reader, I ask you to share your dream with other people in the coming days.

Before you do, stand up right now, raise your arms high above your head, and declare loudly "My dream will come true! My dream will come true! My dream will come true!"

If you practice this process regularly with enthusiasm and conviction, you will be amazed how quickly your dream will be manifested.

Questions for Reflection

1. What is the dream that is most important to you?

2. When you were vividly imagining your dream coming true, where were you?

3. Who was cheering for you?

Chapter 10

Follow Your Joy

As I've taken this journey through life, I have faced great challenges. There were times when I felt alone and stranded at a crossroad. I didn't know whether to go north, south, east, or west. At those times, I needed guidance. I discovered that following my joy led me where I wanted to go.

Several years ago, I had cancer. I didn't know whether I was going to live or die, so I joined a support group for people with catastrophic illnesses. This may sound very depressing, but it turned out to be one of the most inspiring and uplifting events of my life.

The group leader asked, "Annabel, if you had only one week left to live, what would you do?" I knew the answer right away. I would go skiing. The whole group chimed in, "Then do it now!"

A week later, I flew to Colorado. I took the chairlift to the top of the highest mountain, and I chose the steepest, scariest run.

As I skied down the slope, I fell several times, but I got up every time and skied more. I felt so exhilarated! I knew that if this was my last day to live, this was where I wanted to be.

Three people in my support group helped teach me to let joy be my guide. First, there was Howard, who was the chief executive officer of a major company.

He had been a member of the best country clubs and made a lot of money. He said, "I don't need this group. I only come because my doctor told me to." He did not seem very happy.

A few weeks later, when we asked Howard what he wanted to do with the rest of his life, he said, "I've always wanted to write poetry." We said, "Go for it!" Howard started writing the most beautiful, passionate poetry, which he shared with us.

He said, "I just want to thank you for helping me come back to life again." He was much more joyful and peaceful than when he first came to the group.

Then there was Lois. She had beautiful light brown hair and a perfect figure. She came to the group looking very depressed.

When we asked Lois what she wanted to do with the rest of her life, she said, "I've always wanted to model. But a year ago, I had a breast removed. Now I can't possibly do that." We said, "Lois, why don't you take modeling classes?"

Lois started taking modeling and acting classes, and it was like watching a caterpillar transform into a beautiful butterfly. She began to stand taller. She wore beautiful, colorful clothes, and her smile brightened the room.

One day, she came running into the group and said, "Look, I'm in *Honolulu Magazine*. Finally, I'm living my dream!" She was radiant.

The person I will never forget was Mazie. We called her Amazing Mazie. Mazie was eighty-two-years young. She said, "There is so much I want to do! I want to travel around the world. I want to go back to school. But most of all, I've always wanted to jump out of an airplane.

My husband says, 'Mazie, your job is to take care of me.' My children say, 'Oh, Mom, don't be so silly.' But if I had one day left to live, I'd jump out of an airplane."

Mazie continued, "People talk about having near-death experiences. I've had plenty of those. What I want to do before I die is have a near-life experience!" We said, "Mazie, why don't you take skydiving lessons?" And she did.

Week after week, Mazie came to the group and told us how she was preparing for her first jump. One day, she put her arm around me and said, "Dear, why don't we jump together?" I said, "Mazie, I'm not ready for that much joy!"

The day came for Mazie's graduation, when she was going to jump out of a plane for the first time. The group went out to the airfield to support her. The plane circled in the sky, and then Mazie jumped!

Her parachute burst open. She drifted way to the left, then to the right, and way to the left again. She landed far across the field. But something was wrong. Mazie didn't get up. All we could see was a red and yellow parachute.

We ran out to her, screaming, "Mazie, Mazie, are you okay?" Mazie didn't move. I said, "Mazie, wake up!" Mazie still didn't move. I said, "Mazie, if you don't get up, I'm going to give you mouth-to-mouth resuscitation!"

Mazie sat up. She laughed and laughed. "That was the most thrilling thing I've ever done," she said. "I can't wait to jump again!"

I learned an important lesson from Mazie, Howard, and Lois. When they followed their joy, they all felt better. They might never have realized what really mattered if they hadn't fallen ill and joined the group.

I know now that if I fall down, I'll get right back up again. Life is very precious. We need to focus on our dreams, do what we love to do, and follow our joy.

Questions for Reflection

1. If you had only one week left to live, what would you do?

2. What are you passionate about?

3. What do you love doing?

4. What makes your heart sing?

- Chapter 11 -

Deciding to Live

You are constantly making decisions in your life, whether conscious or unconscious. Your decisions bring good things to you, or negative things. Sometimes your decisions can even make the difference between life or death.

I believe that to achieve your dreams, you must make good and powerful decisions along the way that support your personal dreams and vision.

Imagine being happily married for fifty-four years! What a wonderful celebration that would be! The year my parents reached their fifty-fourth anniversary, we didn't celebrate in a restaurant or hotel. Instead, we gathered in the intensive care unit of Kaiser Hospital in Honolulu.

My seven brothers and sisters and I kept a twenty-four-hour vigil as my dad was kept alive on a respirator. We watched the monitors, massaged his limbs, told him how much we loved him, and prayed. The doctor came in and said, "It would take a miracle for your father to come back."

I held my dad's hand, unsure whether he could hear me, and said, "Daddy, do you remember the time you took the whole family hiking on the Summerland Trail at Mt. Rainier?

We were far away from civilization; there were beautiful mountain flowers, patches of snow, and fresh cool air. You chased mountain goats—laughing! That's one of my happiest memories."

Then I said, "Do you remember when I had my senior cello concert at college? You were 3,000 miles away and had to work, so you couldn't make it. It was the first time you ever missed a concert of mine.

You sent yellow roses with a note that said, 'Annabelli, I will always love you.' Daddy, I'm not ready to have you go. I'll never be ready." Our whole family was crying.

Suddenly, the sound of music drifted in. The Hawaiian family in the room next to us was singing Hawaiian songs in an attempt to revive their father. As they sang louder and more jubilantly, their beautiful music lifted our spirits and we felt a new sense of hope. We began to sing Hebrew songs to our father.

Later that afternoon, the doctor came in and unplugged the monitors. My father was breathing on his own. He opened his big blue eyes, looked at us, and said, "I've decided to live!" It was a miracle.

My father was transferred to the regular hospital ward so he could fully recover. He shared a room with Arnold. Arnold had already prepared for his death. He said the price of coffins was just too high these days, so he had built his own.

He laid in it to make sure there was enough room. He put his passport and credit cards in it. His wife said, "Arnold, where you're going, you won't need your credit cards." Arnold replied, "I never leave home without them."

Then he said to my father, "Walter, if you get to heaven, I'll take you out to breakfast." My father said, "Arnold, I've already eaten; besides, I've decided to go home to be with my family."

During the following year, I took wonderful walks with my dad. We'd tell each other stories and jokes. One day I asked my father, "Dad, did you decide to come back to life because you missed us?" He said, "No, I came back to make sure you would all get singing lessons."

Each day, we have the choice. Are we deciding to live, thinking thoughts of hope and joy, being grateful for what we have?

Or are we doing the opposite—being caught up in despair and frustration, living with regrets, thinking thoughts such as, "I wish I had a husband like you have," or "I wish I had kids like yours." Since that day, I decided to be happy with all that I have.

When I think back to my parents' anniversary that day in the hospital room, I realize the family next to us will never know how important their singing was. We just never know how much the songs we sing or the words we speak will lift someone's spirit so they, too, will say, "I've decided to live!"

To achieve our dreams, we must decide to live with joy, passion, and purpose, not only for ourselves but for others we touch along the way.

Questions for Reflection

1. Are your decisions bringing more positive energy into your life or the opposite?

2. Are you deciding to live with joy, zest, and passion?

3. How are you deciding to make your dreams a reality?

Chapter 12

Moving Your Naha Stone

What is getting in the way of making your dreams come true? What is keeping you from taking action to achieve your dreams?

To make our dreams come true, we must take action. If we are feeling physically lethargic, sick, or depressed, it is impossible to achieve our dreams. We must nourish and energize our bodies, minds, and spirits with healthy food, fresh air, exercise, and positive thoughts.

In the Hawaiian language, *ha* means breath or energy. *Ha* is in many important words. *Aloha* does not only mean hello, goodbye, peace, or love. It also means I give you my energy, my life force. *Mahalo* is thank you for giving me your life energy. At the center of our life is our family, our *ohana*, which is at the heart of our life energy. Our extended family or very close friends are *hanai*, where our life energy is shared with people we feel connected to outside of our birth family.

We must do things to energize ourselves with our breath. I love to swim in the gorgeous ocean at Ala Moana Beach. As I stroke through the silky water and come up for air, the deep breathing invigorates my body. Likewise, running by the ocean and deeply breathing in the salty ocean air is very purifying for my mind, body, and spirit. After this wonderful, healthy exercise, I feel radiant and my inner battery is recharged. The ocean always resets my being to a state of vitality and joy!

If I don't have time for a swim or run, I use the *Ha* breath, which is a very fast method to energize your body. I teach the *Ha* breath to my audiences. I ask them to choose a number between one and ten to determine how much energy they have. One is low and ten is high. We then stand, reach our arms high in the air, and together, we quickly pull down our arms, closing our hands into fists as we yell, "Ha!" and exhale from our diaphragms. We do this at least ten times, getting louder and faster. There is always a tremendous amount of excitement as the sound reverberates throughout the room.

I then ask the participants to choose a number again. When I ask who has a higher number, meaning more energy, all hands go up. This exercise demonstrates that we can very quickly transform our bodies into a much happier state within seconds. Then we have more energy to take action and achieve our goals and dreams. You can do the *Ha* breath right now. Go ahead and give it a try.

Over two hundred years ago, a young man lived in Hawaii who had a dream of becoming a leader and doing something truly great with his life. This man was a lesser chief, not of the bloodline required to ascend to the throne, so it seemed impossible that he would become a great leader. He knew he needed to prove his capabilities.

One day, he announced he would lift and move the Naha Stone. Legend has it that whoever could move the sacred Naha Stone possessed the spiritual power to rule the land and unite the Hawaiian Islands. People did not believe he could do this because others stronger and bigger than him had been unable to accomplish this feat. He prepared by vividly imagining himself lifting and moving the stone.

The day came and a large crowd gathered. First the bigger, stronger warriors tried to move the huge stone, but they could not do it. Then it was the young man's turn. As people watched, he began breathing deeply with the *Ha* breath as he energized his body. His eyes bulged and became red and his body appeared to grow in size, as he shouted "Ha!" over and over again, louder and faster.

He reached down, and calling on the power of the gods, lifted and moved the Naha Stone! This young man became King Kamehameha the Great who went on to unify the Hawaiian Islands. Moving the Naha Stone was the event that demonstrated his greatness and worthiness to ascend to the throne.

My Naha Stone, which for a long time was unmovable, was that I did not feel smart enough. I did not think I was intelligent in the academic, brilliant sense, but I wanted to prove to myself and others that I was smart.

I had heard about Harvard University's John F. Kennedy School of Government. I very much wanted to attend its one-year Master's Degree Program in Public Administration because Harvard has the image of being one of the best schools in the world, so people assume you are brilliant if you go there. It is very difficult to get accepted. My deep, heartfelt reasons for wanting to attend were to prove to myself that I was smart and to be part of something very prestigious.

One requirement for acceptance was to score high on the GMAT standardized test. I had never done well on SAT tests, but I took the Kaplan preparation course and studied very hard so I would do well.

When I received the test results, I sobbed. My score was much lower than what was expected for entrance into Harvard. I thought, *Well, this is the end of that dream.*

In the midst of my tears and feeling like a failure, I remembered Harvey Williams, my high school biology teacher. After I graduated from high school, a parent told me Mr. Williams had said, "Annabel Chotzen is the most brilliant student I have ever had."

I thought I was dreaming, so years later I visited him and asked, "Is that true? Did you really say that?" Mr. Williams said, "Yes, that is true; you were my most brilliant student." I should have asked him why he said that. I don't remember doing anything out of the ordinary. That memory gave me the courage to continue to pursue my dream.

Even now when I feel challenged technically and my husband and son become frustrated trying to get me to understand technical things, I remember Harvey Williams. No one is good at everything, but each of us has brilliance in something. Believe that you are a shining, brilliant human being and make your dreams come true!

I learned there would be a recruitment meeting and the admissions director of Harvard's Kennedy School would be coming to Seattle. Something inside of me said, "Don't give up yet," so I attended the meeting. I walked up to the admissions director—a lovely, tall, slender woman with silver hair and deep blue eyes—and said, "My name is Annabel Chotzen. I have accomplished a lot of great things in the community. I got very low scores on my GMAT exam, but I would really love to be accepted into your program."

A couple of days later, she called me and said, "Pack your bags. You need to be in Cambridge in two weeks. You've been accepted into the program with a scholarship." I was amazed and thrilled!

I had to figure out a quick way to come up with the money to attend Harvard. The scholarship only covered a small percentage of the tuition, living, and travel expenses. And now I would have to quit my job at the Seattle Planning Commission, my only source of income. I considered options. Perhaps I could pay some portion of the tuition with loans.

I considered selling my beloved bright red, shiny Toyota Corolla with a sunroof. Why I had a sunroof in Seattle is unexplainable, but the sun does shine there occasionally.

A friend of mine, Dale, the head of the city's purchasing department, worked close by. He was a big man with a husky voice and gray hair who was having health challenges. I liked him and we often chatted.

When I told him I was leaving to go to Harvard, his eyes filled with tears. Even though I did not mention I was going to sell my car, Dale said, "Annabel, I want to buy your car for my daughter."

I told him how much I had decided to sell it for, and then I asked, "When would you and your daughter like to drive it and take it to a mechanic?" Dale replied, "I don't need to drive it or have it checked out. I know you. You take good care of things."

Then he took out his checkbook and wrote a check for the full amount. The next day, Dale arrived with his daughter and she drove away in her beautiful, shiny red car. With the money, I was able to fund my year at Harvard.

One thing I learned after applying to Harvard was that they accept one in three applicants to their graduate school.

I was surprised by this, expecting the competition to be much tougher, but because many people think they are not smart enough to be Harvard students, they never apply. Others think they don't have enough money, but the opportunities are there.

People always come up with reasons for not following their dreams. "I am too young, too old, not pretty enough, not rich enough, not smart enough." Is it possible that maybe they don't *really* want that dream?

Maybe they don't really want that special life partner, a wonderful highly paid job, or an opportunity to attend Harvard. Maybe they *kind of* want something, but they don't want it enough to do what it takes.

In order to achieve our dreams, we must *really, really want them to come true*. And we must know ourselves well enough to know what we truly want. Successful people don't blame their outer circumstances if they face obstacles. They find a way to make their dreams come true anyway.

And if for some reason that dream does not come true after they have done everything possible, they can see the gift. There is something even better for them. I believe that every good effort is rewarded.

I was thrilled to become a student at the John F. Kennedy School of Government at Harvard University. However, it was not always easy. Many of the students came from very different backgrounds. Some were military officers.

My parents, Holocaust survivors, had become peace activists in America. They felt so fortunate to be alive and wanted to help others "find their freedom." As a child, I attended peace rallies. When I was five years old, I gave my first speech. I stood on a stage surrounded by mothers holding peace signs and crying babies. I spoke confidently. "Bombs are bad for kids and other living things." I bowed and everyone cheered. I was hooked on public speaking from that moment on.

At the Kennedy School, I sat in classes alongside military officers. We got into some heated discussions. Ingrained in me from childhood was the belief that all weapons were bad.

My mind was closed, and I just repeated my position, unwilling to yield. In frustration, one officer said, "Annabel, you don't belong in the School of Government. You should be in the Divinity School." I went home and cried.

Subsequently, I was informed that I would be required to take a course taught by the conservative commentator William Kristol called "The Ethics and Morals of Nuclear Weapons."

Like a conscientious objector, I marched into the dean's office and said, "I cannot take this class. Nuclear weapons have no ethics and morals." The dean told me that if I wanted to graduate and get my Master's degree, I had no choice. I wanted to graduate so I changed my mind and attended the class.

Professor Kristol, now familiar with my disdain for the subject, gave me an assignment to write an analytical paper and give a presentation to the class answering the question "Would I use a weapon if I could save one person's life?"

Through this assignment, I realized that under certain circumstances, I, too, would use a weapon. I also gained great respect for our military personnel who selflessly put their lives on the line "to help others find their freedom"— the same goal my parents had.

Due to this mind-broadening experience, I was able to become less biased and more compassionate for people with different points of view. After returning to Hawaii, I had the opportunity to teach military students and give presentations to military groups. If I had not learned valuable lessons from Professor Kristol, this never would have happened.

The more we listen to and understand other people, the more doors of opportunity will open for us and the faster we will achieve our goals and dreams.

As for me, I had moved my Naha Stone. It wasn't easy, but the desire to accomplish my goal was much greater than my fear of failing. That is what motivated me and kept me focused on my dream. Energize yourself, move your Naha Stone, and take action to achieve your dreams.

Questions for Reflection

1. What is your Naha Stone that you need to lift and move out of the way?

2. What actions do you need to take to be able to move your Naha Stone?

3. Was there someone who said negative things who made you believe you could not achieve your dreams? What did they say? Are you repeating those same words to yourself today?

4. Was there a person who said positive things, who made you believe you are unique and special? What did they say? Whose voice are you listening to today?

5. How can you listen to and understand other people's points of view in a new and different way?

Chapter 13

Connecting and Disconnecting

Life is precious and short. Those who succeed in making their dreams come true have learned an important secret: Connect with what is working and brings results and disconnect from what is not working and does not bring results. This is actually a simple concept, but for many people, it is very difficult to implement.

Something about human nature causes people to keep doing the same things over and over again even when the results are not good. They remain stuck in unhealthy relationships that are not truly fulfilling because they do not think they deserve anything better or because they are comfortable with that person or way of life.

Only when there is a drastic life or death situation will people say, "I better change or something serious could happen." I've seen that many people will keep doing the same things or keep hanging out with the same people even when it does not make them happy or bring them closer to their true heartfelt dreams.

When I was growing up in a large family, my household job was vacuuming. Now as a wife and mother in a small family, I still vacuum. On a regular basis, I get satisfaction from plugging in the vacuum, hearing the roar as it sucks up the dirt, and then having a beautiful, clean house.

When I turn off the vacuum cleaner, there is silence once again. In the same way, when I switch on a lamp, the light turns on, and when I switch it off, the light instantly goes off. These two activities create a powerful, yet simple image that I carry with me.

When something does not feel right in my heart, I disengage quickly and unplug from the unhappy situation causing discontent simply by choosing to switch it off.

When a person or situation feels bright and light, I want to interact with that person and plug into that situation.

Here is a good question to ask yourself: Is this situation or person bringing me peace of mind and happiness, or is it causing me to feel unhappy and not good about myself?

Sometimes, we will choose to disconnect for a short period of time, renew ourselves, and then reenter the situation. At other times, we will disconnect for days, or even permanently, if we decide that person or situation is not beneficial to our desire to have a healthy, happy life of pursuing and living our dreams.

To make your dreams come true, you need to surround yourself and connect with people who believe in you and want to help you. These people should be uplifting for your spirit and be people you admire and respect.

Any impediments must be removed in order for you to achieve your dreams. All you have to do is consciously choose to disconnect and switch off the person or situation that is in your way.

Questions for Reflection

1. Who or what would you like to connect with to achieve more of what you want?

2. Who or what would you like to disconnect from to get rid of what you don't want?

3. What is keeping you from taking these actions?

Chapter 14

Discovering the Authentic You

I believe we are much more likely to achieve our greatest dreams if we love and accept the unique person we are, rather than trying to please others and be someone we are not. One of life's biggest challenges is discovering who we really are and loving everything about ourselves. It is a lifetime challenge.

I remember junior high being very difficult because we were all trying to fit in. We all wanted to be liked, accepted, and not stand out. When I was in the seventh grade, we had a student newspaper. In one issue, students voted for the best this and the best that. I was voted "best legs."

After this was published, a female classmate came up to me and said, "It was all a joke because your legs are really not pretty at all." I was embarrassed and my feelings were hurt. I believed what she said and started wearing longer skirts to cover my legs. This episode affected how I felt about my legs for a long time.

Before attending college, I lived for a year and a half in Israel, traveled through Europe visiting museums, and then enrolled at Bennington College in Vermont where I took a sculpture class.

We had to create figures out of clay, so I tried to copy what I had seen in the museums. My small figurines were perfectly formed, sort of like Barbie dolls, with impressive proportions and long, slender legs.

The sculpture teacher, a hip man from New York, observed what I had crafted and said firmly, "Annabel, this isn't you." I tried again and again, class after class. Each time he said, "Be yourself; don't copy something else. This isn't you."

After a few weeks of this rejection, I was furious and had trouble sleeping. One night, I had a dream that I was walking with a large group of people.

We approached a huge concrete wall. There was no way we could climb over it, but I ran and miraculously leaped over it, accomplishing what seemed impossible!

My dream awakened me, so I got out of bed and went to the sculpture studio. I took a bunch of clay and threw it down on a board on the ground. Then I took more clay and slammed that on top.

Pretty soon, I had a huge mound of clay. I began to create this humongous woman with hair standing straight up, big bulging eyes, a huge fat belly, large arms stretched up in the air, and huge thighs. I took a large paint brush and slapped bright red paint over every inch of her.

I still wasn't finished. I dipped a broad brush in a can of shellac and brushed it generously over the red coat of paint. Now I had created a huge, red, bright shiny woman creature.

Suddenly, I felt something wonderful release itself inside me. It was such a cathartic experience. In some way, I felt that this bright, red, outrageous woman was the real me.

I had always tried to be liked, tried to do things the right way, but now something was stirring in my soul. I went back to my dorm, went to bed, and slept incredibly peacefully.

The next day, I went to my sculpture class. As I walked in, I heard the students laughing as they looked at the large red creature in the center of the room.

Then the teacher came in. There was total silence. He walked slowly, circling the red lady several times. Then he said, "Who made this?"

I was so scared I was shaking. I was afraid if he found out I had made that creature, he would flunk me and I might even get expelled. I couldn't bring myself to speak. I didn't say a word. "Who made this?" he said louder. I still didn't say a word. His voice thundered, "Who made this?" In a very soft voice, I squeaked, "I did." He declared, "*This…is a masterpiece!*"

I could not believe what I had heard. I was amazed. I felt extremely proud. I felt that this outrageous red woman was me, the me who had never revealed herself before.

I was courageous and strong; my arms could stretch to do impossible things; I could leap over walls. This was the real me, the woman I wanted to be, not the slender, perfect image of models in magazines.

The teacher wanted to buy my masterpiece and take it back to New York, but I wanted to keep it, so I told him proudly, "This woman is not for sale."

I carried the red lady on my lap on the plane all the way home to Seattle. The flight attendant smiled and said, "I see you have a nice traveling companion." The man seated next to me wanted to buy her! I said emphatically, "She is not for sale."

I arrived home, and while moving my masterpiece, she slipped out of my hands, crashed to the floor, and splintered into hundreds of pieces. I fell to my knees, trying to see how I could reconstruct her, tears streaming down my cheeks.

Realizing there was no way to put her back together, I felt a part of me had shattered with her. However, I had learned an important lesson: To achieve my dreams, I had to be who I really was. I had to be the authentic me.

Now I am truly happy to be me with my healthy body and legs. Legs that have run a marathon, legs that have skied the mountains of Sun Valley, Aspen, Telluride, Jackson Hole, Alta, and Taos.

Legs that kick as I swim in the Hawaii ocean. Legs that dance in the moonlight with my husband hugging me. My legs are perfect just the way they are! I am perfect exactly the way I am!

Do not try to copy someone else. Be true to yourself. Each one of us is a unique, valuable masterpiece!

Questions for Reflection

1. In what ways do you attempt to fit in with everyone else? Does this prevent you from being the true, authentic you?

2. What is unique about you?

3. How can you give more of your gifts to the world?

4. What is keeping you from being all you can be?

- Chapter 15 -

Helping to Fulfill Others' Dreams

We are the product of the hopes and dreams of previous generations, and we help make dreams come true for future generations. We are all dream makers or dream breakers. We get to choose in each moment. The words we use count, the thoughts we think count, and the actions we take matter.

My parents, Walter and Carla, escaped death from the Nazis in Germany. Being a child of Holocaust survivors is daunting. Many of my relatives died in gas chambers.

It was such a shock to hear these accounts as a young child. My parents' fear of extermination was passed on to me. I had a deep-seated fear that people were out to get me, and sometimes they were.

From the time he was a little boy, Walter had a dream of living in America. When he finally escaped Germany, it was a life or death matter. Had he not been successful, neither I nor my siblings, my son, nor my nephews and nieces would be here today.

Walter worked tirelessly to start over in a new country and to give his children the opportunities to make their dreams come true.

Carla's dream was to have lots of children. Because of that, I was so lucky to have been born along with seven spectacular brothers and sisters. I love being part of this large family!

My parents encouraged all of us to follow our dreams. "Whatever it is you want, you can have it. Go for your dreams. Do not wait."

Although my parents were not wealthy, they provided me with cello lessons, took us skiing, and sent me to Bennington College in Vermont. They always said, "Reach for your dreams and the ways and means will follow."

Now, as a mother, I am encouraging my son Devin to follow his dreams. He has many gifts, including a brilliant mind. One time, Will and I met with his four teachers and two school counselors. We wanted to know how Devin was doing in school and how we could support him to be happier.

We were concerned that he might be antagonizing other students because he talked about not being liked and having no friends. Yet what we heard from his teachers was different.

"Devin is liked and respected by the students. He is a leader who is admired. He has a great sense of humor." We were amazed and thrilled by their comments. His teachers affirmed his strengths and gifts.

Too often, we only see our faults and fail to realize the way others perceive us. If we knew how other people felt about us, it might surprise us and improve our self-confidence.

As Devin's mother, it is my most important job to help him feel good about himself, in his own soul. I am passing on to him what I have learned.

Questions for Reflection

1. What were your parents' dreams?

2. How did you help to fulfill their dreams? How did they help to fulfill yours?

3. What dreams do you have for your children or for future generations?

4. What are you doing to help fulfill their dreams?

Chapter 16

Spiritual Guides Help Us

Asking for help is essential to the process of putting your dreams to work. Great therapists can help us discover what is holding us back as well as teach us to use positive visualizations and meditation. We must search until we find the teachers and helpers who resonate with us and give us unconditional support.

Although we are responsible for taking the steps to reach our dreams, special people show up in our lives who provide us with precious wisdom and valuable guidance.

I have had wonderful counselors and therapists who have helped me heal from painful experiences, and I have discovered inspirational spiritual leaders from different faiths.

There is one person, Reverend Allie Diehl, a Religious Science minister, whom I credit with moving me forward to achieve my dreams. When I would meet with Reverend Allie, she would ask me what it was I most desired.

After I told her, she would close her eyes and perform a spiritual mind treatment. She would begin by saying, "There is only one power and one presence active in this universe. It is God, the Good Omnipotent. God is love, God is health, God is peace, God is prosperity. I, Annabel, am one with this one power and one presence."

She would then proceed to speak words as if the dream had already been accomplished; for example, seeing me in perfect health with all that I hoped for.

Reverend Allie taped these sessions so I could listen to them over and over. Her vision of my future became so much a part of my consciousness that I deeply believed I could accomplish these dreams.

Let us admit that many times when we want something, we tend to whine and focus on what we lack. I learned from Reverend Allie that whatever we focus on, we get more of.

For example, if we focus on scarcity, we will continue to have scarcity. On the other hand, focusing on our dreams as if they have already come true will clearly lead us toward realizing them.

Focusing on my dreams as if they had already come true was powerful. I could feel, taste, see, and believe the truth deep within my being.

Learning this method from Reverend Allie significantly shaped my life. The people who helped me reach my goals were those who believed in my dreams.

My husband, Will, is a perfect example. He is my miracle maker. Will became my best friend after knowing me for only a few weeks. He believed in my dreams and helped make them come true.

Surround yourself with people who believe in your dreams. Let go of the people who don't. One phrase I like for letting go of things that hinder me is, "I release this thought, person, or idea into the nothingness from whence it came."

Connect with what you want more of, and release what is not working in your life. Time is precious. Life is precious. Do it now!

Questions for Reflection

1. Who believes in your dreams whom you can enlist to help you?

2. Who or what do you need to let go of so your dreams can gain momentum?

- Chapter 17 -

Overcoming Hardships

We have all been mistreated at some point in our lives by another person. Often, we think we are responsible and feel a sense of shame or guilt. We may feel like a bad or undeserving person.

We may think, "I'm a failure. It's my fault that those things happened." Those voices tell us we're not good enough or worthy enough to achieve our dreams.

In order to take action to achieve our dreams, we need to overcome those painful times in our lives and believe in ourselves again. Ultimately, we must reach a point where another person's actions or words no longer affect how we feel about ourselves.

We may still remember the incident, but we are shining such a bright light of joy, peace, and happiness that the darkness is dissolved.

When feelings of anger and sadness arise, we need to let go of them in appropriate ways. For example, we can pound pillows or yell in the car, as long as no one else can hear us. Running and swimming are also wonderful ways of physically releasing pent-up feelings.

We can also make a decision to focus on what it is we want more of and not give attention to any unhappy, dark thoughts. If we count our blessings and name them one by one, we will feel immense gratitude for all we have.

When we realize that those who hurt us are not better than us, but are in fact the opposite, we will see them as small in size, dimension, and demeanor. They will no longer have power over us.

When we feel our own greatness, then we can achieve our dreams. We will be able to make the inner decision that we deserve the best and that nothing and no one can stop us from achieving our good. We will be empowered to go for our dreams! No more excuses of poor me. Knowing that we are worthy, we can move forward to achieve exactly what we want in our precious lives.

For almost a decade, I worked in a government position where people I served held a great deal of power. I enjoyed my job and received excellent evaluations. However, things began to change when I got a new supervisor.

He would call me into his office and swear at me. He did not understand the work I was professionally trained in, and he commanded me to do things his way.

I went to the head of the organization to speak about this situation and request I be assigned to a new supervisor.

Instead, I was told, "If anyone can handle this person, you can."

About the same time, a powerful member of the committee I reported to complained about my work performance and called for an investigation. I was not allowed to return to my office or do any work and was relegated to a small room with only a desk and a telephone.

I sent a note to the head of the organization, imploring, "Please, just let me do my job." There was never any response. I felt grief-stricken and devastated when it became apparent that no one was going to help me clear up this situation.

Sitting alone in that small room, I decided to call a motivational speaker I knew. Jerry Coffee, who had been a prisoner of war for seven years in Vietnam, answered my call, listened to my plight, and was very kind in his response.

"Annabel," he said, "use this experience to understand the pain other people are going through. When you speak to your audiences, you will have more compassion than ever before."

I also called Kent Keith, a friend of my husband, who wrote "The Paradoxical Commandments," which Mother Teresa had placed on a wall in her children's home in Calcutta.

In his book by the same name, Kent talks about a time when he was kicked out of college, taken at night to a bus stop, and abandoned there. I knew Kent would understand the pain I was feeling, and he was incredibly supportive.

In time, I found a courageous attorney who helped me exit as gracefully as possible from this terrible situation. For a long time, I felt I was a failure—shamed and disgraced. At first, it was difficult for me to leave the house because I was afraid I would run into one of those powerful people.

I began to look around me and noticed that when people are immersed in grief and disappointment for a long period of time, they often get sick and even die. I loved life and was determined to pull myself out of this morass.

I began to focus on what I really wanted in my life…to feel joy and to use this painful experience to help other people achieve their own bliss.

I worked with my amazing spiritual counselor, Reverend Allie. She kept asking me, "What is it that you want?" When I replied, we would close our eyes and vividly imagine that dream coming true.

She spoke words of truth and made audio recordings that I listened to several times a day while in a deep state of relaxation. I also took action to pursue what I wanted—to become a motivational speaker.

Thereafter, whenever I spoke to audiences at meetings and conventions, I felt a sense of power as I helped people focus on achieving their dreams. I counted my blessings, including having additional time to play with my two-year-old son and spend more quality time with my husband.

With time, my self-esteem, dignity, and belief in myself were restored. I had made the decision that nothing could stop me from my good, and that the source of good in my life was not a person in a powerful position. It is God.

Now and then, I would wake up in the middle of the night because I'd had a nightmare. I would get up, breathe deeply, and count one hundred blessings in my life.

Sometimes, I sat in front of a mirror, looked deep into my eyes, and told myself ways that I was a success. Then I would go back to bed and sleep incredibly peacefully. This worked so well that I still do it if I can't sleep.

Throughout my ordeal, I remained true to myself. I knew I had done nothing wrong and had only hoped that the truth would be revealed. Now, many years later, those powerful people seem small and insignificant to me. I have no more shame and they have no more power over me.

Knowing that I am worthy, I hold my head high, smile, and go anywhere without fear of seeing those people who seemed so powerful before.

I am the person I have always wanted to be…a wife, the mother of a beautiful child, and a successful motivational speaker who is living in paradise.

I am kind, compassionate, and honest. I am truly happy, focused with gratitude on all that I have, and living my dreams each day!

Although I had the help of a therapist and spiritual counselor, as well as the support of my husband and friends, the most important factor in my coming to terms with this situation was that I had to accept that I was a person worthy of respect. I had to have faith in myself and erase any doubts that I was a good person. I had to love myself.

Respect and a deep sense of self-worth are not only for the powerful and mighty. Every one of us is equally deserving. Take the critical step of reaching out to those people who can help you climb out of your painful situation. This step is your responsibility. Remember, you are worthy and you deserve respect. Never forget this.

Questions for Reflection

1. Was there a time in your life when you experienced a personal challenge, or are you experiencing one now?

2. Have you overcome the hardship of this experience? If so, take the time now to count the ways it has strengthened

you. Write them down so you won't forget the valuable gifts you received from this painful time.

3. Have you been able to empathize and help another person because of your own struggles?

4. If you are currently experiencing a personal challenge, who can you talk to for encouragement, advice, or counseling?

- Chapter 18 -

Healing Your Relationships

When I was in graduate school studying music at the University of Washington, I would walk across the campus to catch the bus home. One day, a man named Pedro was selling his beautiful pieces of ceramic pottery, which were laid out on the immaculate lawn.

I noticed a large glistening bowl. It was glazed with brown and shades of orange, reminding me of a warm sunset. I thought my mother would love it because it was like her—beautiful, elegant, and one-of-a-kind. But being a low-income college student, I did not think spending the money was the right thing to do.

About ten minutes later, while standing at the bus stop, I knew that bowl was meant for my mom. I raced back to Pedro's display, breathing heavily, my heart pounding, hoping the bowl would still be there. It was!

It became my mother's favorite bowl for many years. She placed it in the center of her dining room table in Seattle. When our family moved across the ocean to Honolulu, some things were broken, but not that gorgeous bowl. It adorned our home.

A few years ago, my mother moved to California. Her new home could only accommodate a few things and the bowl was left behind. Since she cherished the bowl, I brought it to my home to remind me of the special bond it created between us.

Will, Devin, and I recently moved. I placed the bowl in a special place in our lovely, new living room. As Will was hanging a painting on the wall, the painting suddenly slipped from his fingers and fell right onto the bowl.

With a loud crack, the bowl broke into pieces and I burst into tears. Will said, "I'm so sorry! I know how much that bowl has meant to you."

I gathered the broken pieces and placed them in the garbage can, then went to my orchestra rehearsal. One of the blessings of playing music is that it always makes me feel better when I am sad.

A serendipitous moment occurred after I shared my story with a few orchestra friends. One said, "There is a way to fix broken ceramic bowls. I know because my brother is a ceramicist. Just call the Honolulu Museum of Art." The life of the beautiful bowl did not have to end.

I went home, retrieved the pieces from the garbage, and Will placed them all neatly together in the original shape of the bowl. They all fit perfectly like a jigsaw puzzle! It is now ready to be glued together and will become whole once again.

I thought about how the broken pieces are like broken relationships. Perhaps there is someone we cherish who acted without integrity.

Naturally, we lose trust in them and out of hurt, impulsively feel like throwing the relationship away. Instead, is it possible to put the pieces back together, knowing it has been damaged, but still being able to salvage the relationship?

We spend a tremendous amount of energy and time being upset with others who act in objectionable ways. When we focus on disliking people, that energy takes away from moving forward in a positive way to achieve our goals and dreams. Can we accept others unconditionally even after they have hurt us?

There is a Japanese method of repairing broken ceramics called *kintsugi*—filling cracks in bowls with gold, silver, or platinum dust. Instead of trying to repair the bowl so that the cracks are invisible, the metallic dust fills the cracks and makes it even more beautiful than the original. The cracks symbolize the broken relationships, and the beautiful metallic dust symbolizes healing.

The Indian philosopher Rumi said, "The wound is where the light enters." Without wounds and cracks, there would be no way for light to enter and strengthen us.

We learn and grow from the painful things that happen to us. I have heard that when a bone breaks, it is stronger than before it was broken once it has healed.

I am visualizing the bowl, which symbolizes my soul filled with light entering through the cracks of hurt and pain. I will strive to forgive, continue to love, and engage with others in healthy ways.

I encourage you to become aware of the cracks in your relationships and still see the good in each person.

That does not mean you have to engage with people who have hurt you, but you will be filled with a healthy sense of peace and tranquility if you value the lessons you learned from those painful situations. Then no one can hold you back from achieving your dreams.

Questions for Reflection

1. Do you have relationships that are cracked and in need of mending?

2. Can you acknowledge the pain and accept the cracks?

3. How will mending relationships help to make your dreams come true?

Chapter 19

Following Your Dreams
Despite Setbacks

When I was a little girl, my parents took me to the Seattle Symphony. At one concert, world famous Pablo Casals was playing the cello. I couldn't believe the incredible sounds that reverberated throughout the concert hall.

As I sat in my chair, my small legs hanging over the edge of the seat far from the ground, I knew I wanted to play the cello.

My mother, Carla, was a gifted pianist. She had auditioned and was accepted with a scholarship to the Eastman School of Music, but she never went there because she decided to get married and soon had eight children.

When I was a child, I would listen to her play beautiful Mozart sonatas on our baby grand piano with tears streaming down her cheeks. I always felt like she was missing her parents who lived far away, or her relatives who were killed in gas chambers in Germany.

One of Carla's dreams was to have enough children to have a string quartet, but instead, she got eight children with plenty of strings attached.

The oldest were twins, Vonny and Danny. They played viola and violin. They practiced dutifully, but they quit after a while. Of all the eight children, I was the only one who had a passion for music and continued to play an instrument.

In the third grade, when my teacher was handing out instruments, I said, "I want to play the cello." He said my hands were too small and gave the cello to my friend Tina.

But one day, Tina quit, so I said again, "I want to play the cello." That first day when I carried it home, it was larger than I was. And then I found out a terrible thing. I would have to practice.

I practiced for hours, days, and years. My friends would stick their heads in my bedroom window and say, "Annabel, can you come out and play?" and I would say, "In a little while; I have to practice."

I graduated early from Garfield High School in Seattle, Washington. It was the '60s and dangerous to be white in a black ghetto.

When Stokely Carmichael spoke at one of our assemblies, I felt anger pouring out of his soul. The crowd cheered and I rushed home to safety.

A lot of hostility was being directed toward white people. For example, my mother was going to buy a house for a community art center, but before the deal closed, it was burned down.

My high school counselor encouraged me to graduate early, in January instead of June, because of the potential danger for white people in the inner city of Seattle.

A few months later, I took my cello and left for a kibbutz in Israel; then I attended the Hebrew University in Jerusalem. I would practice when I could, and later auditioned and was accepted to play with the Haifa Symphony.

But the people on the kibbutz told me they would not let me play because everyone on the kibbutz was expected to do the same things. We worked in the orchards in the morning and studied Hebrew in the afternoons.

"We won't let you play in the Haifa Symphony," they said. Israel is a Socialist country. Everyone gets health care and is fed, but there are few opportunities for people to reach for their own personal dreams.

I was very sad that I was not allowed to play my cello with the Haifa Symphony. When I went to the doctor, there were lines of people waiting and it took the whole day to be seen.

On top of that, there were no hamburgers, no peanut butter sandwiches, and I missed America. In America, you may succeed or you may fail, but you have the opportunity to follow your dreams.

Fourteen months later, on my way home to America, I auditioned at the London Conservatory of Music, and I couldn't believe it—I was accepted! I could become a really good cellist!

But I really, really missed America. I agonized over my decision of whether to stay in London and study cello at a prestigious conservatory of music or to return to America where I had left my heart.

I decided to go to Bennington College instead—a school in Vermont well-known for creativity and brilliant instructors in the arts. My senior cello recital included my own compositions, playing a solo with a small orchestra, and playing a Bach unaccompanied cello suite.

After I graduated, I returned to Seattle to attend the University of Washington, studied conducting, and received my teaching certificate in music. I also continued to study the cello.

I decided I wanted to study with the woman who was considered the best cello teacher in Seattle. She had been in a concentration camp, a number printed on her arm. When she played, she looked like she was in pain.

Often, she yelled at her students, and some of them quit playing. I thought she was so angry because she had been persecuted in the concentration camp.

But I was determined to be the best cellist I could be, so I persuaded my parents to pay for lessons, even though I was told by other students, "You might quit and end up hating the cello," I proceeded to study with this woman, believing she would help me refine my skills the way fire smooths metal.

Technically, she was excellent. Unfortunately, I was a sensitive young woman and no match for the rage that spewed from this teacher. Once she yelled, "You will never amount to anything!" I became very nervous, developed a fear of performing, and lost my love of playing the cello.

You must understand that I had always loved the cello. It was a friend I had grown up with. I would embrace my cello, draw the bow across the strings, and a beautiful voice would respond.

Over time, my love rekindled and I would occasionally still play chamber music or practice on my own. When you deeply love someone or something, the love remains.

I wrestled with the trauma I had suffered. But I loved music so much that gradually I fell in love with playing the cello again. Each time I embraced my cello and drew the bow across the strings, hearing the wonderful, deep, harmonious sounds, a deep feeling of gratitude and joy encompassed my being.

My joy of playing returned just as a bright light always overcomes darkness. Keep doing what you love and you, too, can dig yourself out of your dark pit and embrace the light.

One lesson I have learned is it is far better to be technically less proficient with a high level of love and passion than be subjected to a tormented human being.

Following our dreams does not mean putting ourselves in compromising, dangerous situations of body, mind, and spirit.

And there were others, far more compassionate and loving, who could have given me lessons in technique. Seek out mentors and teachers who lift you up while still demanding the best from you.

I play the cello now with tremendous joy! Last night, when I was playing the unaccompanied Bach Suite in C major, some of the passages made my heart soar!

I am so fortunate that Devin enjoys playing the cello too. My husband and our orange kitty Kalika (meaning silky in Hawaiian) love the sound of the cello. My husband Will says over and over, "I wish you would play more. It sounds so beautiful!" Today, I play in an orchestra in Hawaii with some outstanding musicians.

With my handsome son launched, my beautiful husband following his dream of doing good and succeeding, living with my family in paradise in Hawaii, swimming in the gorgeous ocean, speaking at conventions in the most beautiful luxury hotels in the world, and now playing music again, I am truly living all of my dreams!

To achieve your dreams, remember to always do what brings you joy. You must practice and feel passionate about what you are doing!

Questions for Reflection

1. What setbacks have kept you from achieving your dreams?

2. Did you give up?

3. How can you reignite those dreams and make them come true?

Chapter 20

Pushing Through Fear

Many people have dreams, but they are afraid to pursue them. While fear can be a good protector, it also can be a barrier to achieving dreams. To go for what we really want, we must push through fear. When we push through fear in any area of our life, it can empower us to face our fears in other parts of our life.

When my students are afraid to stand and deliver speeches, I ask them to close their eyes and vividly imagine something they love doing. Maybe it is horseback riding, or swimming in the ocean, or playing with a child.

Then I ask them to take that same joy and imagine they are giving a speech. When they transfer their positive energy to the thing that makes them scared, the fear dissipates quickly and joy replaces fear.

I then ask each of them to tell a story about their life that brings them a feeling of personal contentment. Once they begin to share their experiences, it is easy for them to speak because they are sharing something they know.

Many of my experiences of moving through fear happened in the mountains on the ski slopes. When I was a young girl, my parents would sometimes take us skiing at Mt. Baker.

At that time, Mt. Baker was undeveloped, so there were only a few skiers. I had some private lessons with Franz Gable, the Olympic Gold Medalist from the Austrian Olympics. He was a jovial man with a warm voice and a strong Austrian accent.

During one lesson, I came to a very steep slope. Franz had skied down to the bottom of the hill and then turned, looking up at me. I was immobilized with fear. The snow was deep. Franz yelled, "Annabel, you can do it!"

I shouted, "I can't do it. I am scared." Franz yelled again, "Annabel, you can do it!" I shouted back, "Call the ski patrol. They can take me down in a toboggan." Franz yelled, "That's for injured people. You are perfectly fine. You can do it!"

Something about his strong, confident voice made me plant my ski poles in the deep snow and push off down the mountain.

I bent my knees, twisting my hips to make turns, like a dancer rhythmically going up and down, back and forth, exhilarated with each movement, the cold air stinging my face, my fingers snug in warm mittens.

When I reached the bottom of the hill, Franz had a big smile and exclaimed, "See, you did it." I said, "Let's do it again!"

To this day, when something scares me, I see Franz Gable on the ski slope in the deep snow yelling, "Annabel, you can do it!"

When I was searching for the man of my dreams, I would choose a ski resort and fly from Hawaii. Flying sometimes made me scared, too, especially when there was a lot of turbulence.

It didn't help that the pilot came back to see me one time to tell me everything would be fine. I told him emphatically, "Go back to the cockpit and fly this plane."

I pushed through my fear and traveled on my own to Alta, Utah; Taos, New Mexico; Jackson Hole, Wyoming; Sun Valley, Idaho; Squaw Valley, California; Aspen, Colorado; Telluride, Colorado; and more.

If I could push through my fear, flying from Hawaii to an unknown place, make friends, take lessons, and ski down those steep slopes, I knew I could do anything.

One time, when I was a young girl skiing with my mother, I looked down at the bottom of a steep hill and was terrified. "There is no way I can get down this," I murmured with a trembling voice.

My mother smiled and said, "It's easy. It's just like having a baby." Well, I had heard that having babies could be difficult and painful. But my mother enjoyed giving birth. She had eight babies and would have had more if my dad had given her the green light. So I trusted her, imagined

I was having a smooth delivery, and made it down the mountain with ease.

Another time, I was on the chairlift with my mother in the middle of a blizzard. The snow was pounding on our faces. I was feeling cold and fearful.

My mother said, "Enjoy the massage as the snow hits your face." My mother's approach to facing fear by always seeing the good in a situation has stuck with me.

And one other thing—she often had small, frozen pecan pies in her ski parka. When she would tear off a piece for me to eat, the sweet nutty pie always gave me extra energy. I loved those little frozen pecan pies, and I have been looking for them ever since the ski days with my mother.

To achieve our dreams, we must face our fears.

Questions for Reflection

1. What experiences in your life have given you the courage to overcome fear?

2. If you hadn't felt afraid, what things would you have done?

3. What fears are keeping you from achieving your dreams now?

4. What actions can you take to push through your fears?

Chapter 21

Gratitude Brings Dreams Closer

Often, people wait until they are in a state of utter despair before deciding to make changes. They see the bad situation they are in, and they finally say they want something else.

When we are focusing on how bad we feel and how difficult things are, it is very difficult—almost impossible—to reverse the tide.

When we are in a state of joy and gratitude, feeling the abundance in our lives, more good comes to us. Whatever we focus on, we get more of.

If we are focusing on the lack of what we want, we are unlikely to create what we do want. If we are focused on how rich and abundant our lives are now, we are likely to receive more riches and abundance.

I live in a mountainous area on Oahu called Tantalus, which overlooks Honolulu. I look over the lovely lighted city at night, the serene blue ocean during the day, and enjoy incredible sunrises and sunsets of pink and orange at dawn and dusk.

We are surrounded by huge, magnificent monkey pod trees, as well as mango, plumeria, and many other lush trees in this beautiful location.

Every morning, we are greeted by the incredibly beautiful songs of the Shama Thrush. We also see green parrots, red-crested cardinals, and many other birds.

The birds sing loudly and joyously as they greet the new day. They are happy to fly around and enjoy the thrilling beauty of being alive. Their lives seem fulfilled and effortless.

When we are in a state of singing our wonderful songs, spreading our wings, and flying toward our dreams, rather than worrying about what anyone else thinks, we are allowing our most magnificent dreams to unfold. By having gratitude, we notice that today we are living many of our past dreams.

I am living my dream of having a wonderful soul mate who nurtures, loves, honors, and respects me as I do him. I dreamed of having a child and gave birth to Devin. Devin has surpassed my wildest dreams because he is brilliant, handsome, musical, funny, kind, gentle, and loving.

From the time I was a little girl in kindergarten in Seattle and the teacher brought each student shells from her visit to Hawaii, I had dreamed of living in Hawaii.

And here I am, having lived in paradise for more than thirty years now! I love swimming in the ocean; it always resets my whole being to a tranquil, peaceful, happy dimension. It is a glorious way to live!

I had dreamed of becoming a motivational speaker and making a difference in people's lives. Today, it is such a joy to speak to audiences from all over the world on Oahu, Kauai, Maui, and the Big Island, and to stay in some of the most beautiful hotels in the world.

I receive constant feedback from people who say my workshops and motivational presentations have made a positive difference in the quality of their lives. My dreams have not only come true but have been far surpassed.

I have played solo passages on my cello in an orchestra and conducted. Sometimes when I play certain notes on my cello, my spirit soars with happiness.

I composed music at Bennington College and had a wonderful music recital. And I attended graduate school at Harvard University where I studied with leaders from all over the world!

I could say that all of my dreams have come true, and certainly I am living my dreams. However, to be alive is to keep creating more dreams, setting more goals, climbing more mountains, and reaching out and touching the lives of more people.

And that is easiest to do when we have joy and gratitude, when we are living in each moment, and when we are grateful for all that we have, counting our blessings and naming them one by one.

When we are focused on the joy of what we already have and really treasure our moments with those we love, when our hearts are filled with happiness, the way is open for more of our dreams to come true.

To Do:

1. Write a list of all the things you are grateful for now. Keep adding to the list and read it daily.

2. Disengage from negative people and situations that are not bringing you joy.

3. If there is something negative going on in your life, ask "What's good about this?"

4. Vividly imagine the life you want in great detail. What we focus on, we get more of. Think positively and don't complain, mentally or verbally.

- Chapter 22 -

The Importance of a Support Group

My friend Kalani once told me, "Share your dreams with people who believe in you, and be open to the support that comes. Ask and you shall receive."

I discovered that he was absolutely right. I have been privileged to be part of several groups that have exposed me to hearing and accepting varying viewpoints, helped me to understand myself better, and taught me the value of surrounding myself with people who provide support to me.

The Friday Night Group

When I was a little girl living with my family in Seattle, a group of adults would meet by the fireplace in our living room on Friday evenings. They would discuss their thoughts, visions for the world, goals, and dreams.

I am not sure how this group originally formed, but they were the most important adults in my childhood. Each came from a different background, congregating in our warm living room like honeybees in a honeycomb.

The group included a composer, an engineer, a health food entrepreneur, a carpenter, an artist, and their spouses. My dad, Walter, was the jovial, storytelling humorist. My mother, Carla, kept us all so wonderfully satiated with her baked Pacific Northwest salmon and other delicious refreshments.

These friends thoroughly enjoyed one another's company. The composer played his latest compositions on the piano and we children danced. The crackling fire added delicate harmony to the group's rich laughter. These were cozy, happy times, juxtaposed against the backdrop of cold, rainy Seattle nights.

The adults would share their thoughts. They encouraged each other to stretch beyond the limits of what was the accepted way of thinking and being.

Everyone was free to share ideas—not to debate, but to listen with an open mind. Creativity was the patchwork of this group, and the beautiful quilts that formed were, even for a child like me, lovely to wrap one's thoughts in.

These adults spoke about their goals and dreams, not only for themselves but for the planet. They cared deeply about the world and helping people, not from a place of being a Democrat, Republican, Socialist, Christian, or Jew, but from their common humanity. This was a fertile environment for dreams to be born.

This group clearly influenced my life. It was a model for me of openness, listening, and sharing without judgment. I came to expect that groups would function this way, and though I have not been able to recreate that type of open, trusting, and free atmosphere that I experienced as a child, it remains the ideal I continue to seek.

The Goals Group

When I moved to Hawaii, I attended Calvary by the Sea Lutheran Church. Doug Olsen was an amazing minister who counseled people of all faiths, and I admired his leadership skills. He held a Tuesday evening group, which I attended, where people shared their experiences.

There I met Nancy, who invited me to join her goals group, which was comprised of five women. In this group, we shared our goals and provided feedback to one another. We held each other accountable in a gentle way, checking back at each meeting. If someone asked for advice, we would offer suggestions.

A key to the group's success was that each person had a specific amount of time to be listened to without interruption. Often in groups, one or two people dominate the conversation and others feel left out.

This group helped me understand that getting equal time is critical, whether you are in a family, a team at work, or sharing in a support group.

In our goals group, we would always open and close the meeting with a prayer. I love praying. One significant thing

Nancy prayed for was my dream of meeting a wonderful man and having a baby. Nancy kept praying for me and my dreams. Though it took a long time, my dreams did come true! Prayer is powerful.

The Mastermind Support Group

I recruited a few women students who had taken my MBA class to form a mastermind support group. The concept of a mastermind group was first discussed in Napoleon Hill's book *Think and Grow Rich*.

In the group, participants help one another set and achieve goals, brainstorm ideas, and support each other with honesty, compassion, and respect. A few other women also joined us, and we met every few months for about three years.

Like the goals group, we always divided the time equally among all attendees. Each person set goals for her work and personal life and asked for feedback. We noticed that we achieved our goals quickly as a result of the suggestions and support of creative, mature women who shared ideas and challenged each other.

The Book Group

I believe that God is always present in the midst of our dreams. God often sends angels to help us. Gail and Amy were the angels God sent to me.

I dreamed of writing this book for many years, and I shared my dream with Gail. As the years went by, she encouraged me to work on it and get it done. Gail had helped many people write and publish their books. She generously offered to coach me and Amy through the process.

Gail gave us writing assignments and expected us to produce our very best work. Her high standards challenged and forced us to improve our writing skills. We met every other month to critique our work, review our progress, and determine our next goals.

Without Gail's firm guidance and encouragement, this book never would have been completed. Gail is truly an angel in my life.

Amy is an angel too. She spent many hours editing my book and giving me valuable suggestions. I am so grateful for these two women.

Make Today Count Support Group

This support group for people facing life threatening health challenges was a highlight of my life. We encouraged and supported one another to make the most of each day.

A life lesson for all of us is: follow your dreams and do what you love with the the time you have left on this earth. Make today count!

Support Groups and What It All Comes Down To

Like Kalani advised, I shared my dreams with others who believed in me. Their support provided me with courage and resolve to persevere and take the difficult steps toward achieving my dreams.

Some of our journeys may be long, but the encouragement that comes with healthy support groups can only help us bear the struggles we will face.

Recently, a friend from a suport group told me that she and her husband voted for the presidential candidate I vehemently opposed. Another friend told me she did not even vote for a president. I was shocked by both of these women and seriously contemplated removing them from my contact list.

My son Devin was horrified. "What? You would remove good friends from your list just because of how they voted? That's crazy."

His candid reaction caused me to pause and reconsider my knee-jerk reaction. I thought about my parents' group of friends and how they were open to and accepting of each other's beliefs.

In comparison, here I was, ready to delete these two friends from my contact list and my life simply for having different political viewpoints from my own. I was usurping the very support group ideal I had spent my lifetime seeking.

I wrestled with this situation until I realized I did not want to lose my dear friends. People will not always agree with me, but I need to believe and trust that we are all making the best choices we can at any given time.

Support groups mean just that—support. Support one another; lift each other up. The group will only work for you if you give as much as you take. Join a support group or form your own group. *Me ke aloha!* May all your dreams come true!

Questions for Reflection

1. Who are the angels who have helped you?

2. Can you find a support group you can join to achieve your dreams? Once you find it, join in! If you can't find one, start your own.

3. How can you share your talents, knowledge, and skills to help others reach their potential?

Chapter 23

Enjoying the Dreams
You Are Living Today

When I was a little girl, sometimes my father walked me to school. On those mornings, I felt very special holding his hand. But two blocks before school, I'd let go of his hand and say, "I can walk the rest of the way myself."

One day when I let go of his hand, my father looked down at me and said, "You're ashamed that I'm your father, aren't you?" "No," I retorted.

It was a lie. I was ashamed. Ashamed of his strong foreign accent, ashamed of the way he dressed. He didn't look or act like other fathers. I loved my father. I was proud of my father except when other people were around.

Sometimes after dinner, even when my friends were there, my father extended his hand to my mother, took her in his arms, and danced around the room. He laughed and laughed. I didn't always know what he was laughing about.

I used to love it when my father would take our family hiking in the mountains. One time, my father chased mountain goats up the trail. He looked so free, like he was one of the goats, unencumbered by the daily pressures of life.

My father spoke out for all kinds of causes and wrote letters to the editor of the newspaper. One time, my teacher read one of his letters in front of the whole class. I was so embarrassed.

That evening I said, "Dad, when you write those letters about your causes, do you think you could sign them using a different name?" My father looked disappointed and said, "Annabelli, come here. Sit down. I want to tell you a story that will explain why I write those letters."

"There was a man who lived in a country where people were being tortured and killed just because they were not the same as other people.

One day, the man decided to escape. He took a small glass vial, placed money inside, and dropped it in a can of oil, then hid the can in his car. He drove to the border.

A guard reached for his gun and shouted 'Stop, don't move.' Trembling, the man handed over his papers.

The guard then searched the car for any evidence of an attempted escape. If caught, the man would be executed as many of his friends and family had been.

The guard picked up the oil can, shook it, and heard a rattle from inside. He looked at the man, and their eyes met.

The man's heart was wildly beating as sweat poured out profusely on his forehead. For some unknown reason, the guard put the can down, smiled at the man, and said 'Move on.'

"Annabel, I am that man. That guard's hand, whatever his reason, was my hand to freedom. Had I not escaped, you would not be here today.

I then came to America and met your beloved mother. We shared a common belief, that freedom is a precious gift, but with it comes a great responsibility. We must extend our hands so that other people can find their freedom."

That day, I saw my father in a new light. As time went on, I began to understand why he gave so much compassion and love to the world when he had experienced so much pain.

Some years later, when I went home for a visit, my father and I walked in the park. We heard a child crying. As we walked around the bend, we saw a mother hitting her little girl. I said, "Dad, let's go." He said, "No, we must do something."

He went over to the child, kneeled down, and embraced her. Then he touched the mother's hand and said, "What a beautiful child you have. I know how difficult it can be to be a parent."

The mother smiled back and seemed transformed. As my father and I walked away, I said, "Dad, why didn't you just yell at the woman?" I will never forget what my father said.

"You must love others to create more love in the world and rise above your anger."

As the years passed, my love for my father deepened. Although he grew a little smaller in stature, in my eyes he was the tallest man in the world.

I realize now that, all along, it was my father's hand that was my hand to freedom. He gave me freedom to love other people regardless of appearance.

Oh, how I wish I could go back in time to when I was a little girl. I'd take my father's hand and hold it tightly. This time I would not let go.

We'd walk all the way to school together. I'd bring him into my classroom and introduce him to all the kids and my teacher. I'd proudly say, "This is my father."

But we cannot go back in time. The past becomes dreams we wish we could relive. Cherish your moments with those you love. Make each moment a dream come true! And enjoy the dreams you are living today.

Questions for Reflection

1. What are the dreams you are living today?

2. How can you appreciate the moments with those you love?

3. If you had a few hours to be with a person who has passed on, whom would you choose and what would you do?

4. Who do you want to treasure and spend more time with now who is alive in your life?

When the Dream Changes Form

Several years ago at summer camp, Devin got three rubber bracelets. One was green, the second yellow and red, and the third was black, green, and yellow. He came home wearing the bracelets, which I thought looked kind of silly. When I looked at other boys his age, none of them wore bracelets.

Many young people have body piercings and tattoos, orange and green hair, things I would never have thought appropriate for myself when I was their age. Perhaps I was being old-fashioned to think it wasn't appropriate for Devin to wear those bracelets.

When Devin performed in the orchestra, he looked so handsome. Yet he always wore the rubber bracelets. Then one morning, after strapping on his hiking boots, putting his lunch in his pack, and getting ready to go out the door for the eighth-grade camping trip, Devin took off his bracelets. He didn't say a word.

He just took them off, put them on the dining room table, and marched out the door, carrying a load of camping gear. I felt like crying out, "No, don't take off those bracelets!"

Suddenly, it was as if Devin was shedding childhood right before my eyes; the taking off his bracelets seemed to mean he was leaving the three of us—me, Will, and our cat—behind. I shed some tears after dropping him off at school for his trip.

One weekend, when my husband's favorite team, the San Francisco 49ers, won a game, Devin came in the living room and jumped up and down with joyful glee, celebrating the victory.

Will asked him to stop jumping because the floors were creaking, but I loved his youthful joyfulness and said, "Let him jump! How many more times will he jump up and down like a little boy?"

Thankfully, Devin came back into the living room and jumped up and down once again. One more time for mom's sake. Who knows? It may be the last time.

Change is part of life. Some people have an easier time with change than others. Will always wanted Devin to move forward, to get out of diapers, to take his first steps, to achieve.

Change has always been difficult for me. I still struggle with it, sometimes wishing Devin was still nursing. That's why I teach people how to handle change in challenging times.

We teach people what we need to learn. As a motivational speaker, "How to Handle Change" is one of my most requested topics.

We can achieve a dream and then it changes. Devin is brilliant and grew up so quickly. But he is no longer the baby of my dreams.

Sometimes I wish I still had that darling little baby boy that I dreamed of having. I want him home with me. But as they say, a ship is safe in the harbor, but that is not what ships are for.

As the wonderful minister Doug Olsen said, "Children are meant for export." My dream must now change to that of having a happy, healthy, joyful, successful young man who can sail on his own.

We achieve dreams and then we need new dreams. My dream was to have a baby. I gave birth to Devin. How can Devin, this newly formed human being, become part of my next dream?

As he sets sail and moves on to create a whole new life, one in which he rarely needs his mom, how can I give birth to new dreams of my own? I need to give birth to myself, my next step, my next dream.

Questions for Reflection

1. Have you been able to let go of past dreams and welcome new dreams?

2. How well do you handle change?

3. What is a dream you had that has changed over time?

Chapter 25

Nurturing Yourself

The more we take care of ourselves, the more energy we have to go for our dreams! Following are six tips for nurturing yourself so you are in the best condition to pursue your dreams.

1. Exercise: Moving our bodies is critical for making us feel wonderful. Walking or running in nature every day can be so healing!

It is nice to be a member of a health club, but you can get great exercise by just having a good pair of walking or running shoes and going outdoors. Walking or running in nature while breathing fresh air is a wonderful activity. You will lose weight and feel much better about yourself.

Swimming is one of the best forms of exercise because it is so gentle on the body. I am so lucky to get to swim regularly in the ocean, but swimming pools are great too!

With a health club membership, you can join yoga and muscle-conditioning classes. The instructors, music, and other people in the class are very encouraging.

When others are exercising, too, it is a great incentive to keep going, and a wonderful camaraderie will develop among the participants!

2. Eat delicious, healthy, nourishing, food: As is often said, "We are what we eat." Food is the foundation of good health.

What you eat makes a big impact on how you feel. Choosing to eat healthy, nutritious food will help your body empower you to live your life to the fullest.

There is plenty of good information online that will give you ideas, recommendations, recipes, and meal plans. A healthy, nourished body will energize your dreams.

3. Use affirmations: Affirmations are great to use often. When we repeat positive statements, our minds begin to accept what we hear. I like to say my affirmations three ways, for example:

"I, Annabel, am a great leader."

"You, Annabel, are a great leader."

"Annabel is a great leader."

Another very powerful way to use affirmations is to look in the mirror and tell yourself the ways you are a success and what you are grateful for.

Look deeply into your eyes and smile as if you were speaking to your best friend. After all, you are your best friend. No one can make you feel as wonderful as you can.

4. Breathe: Deep breathing is truly fantastic. It calms us down and centers our minds and spirits. There are many different breathing techniques that you can find information about online.

Personally, I have received much benefit from learning the breathing practices taught by Sri Sri Ravi Shankar through the Art of Living Foundation.

5. Meditate: Meditation is taught by a variety of teachers. Find a technique that works for you. My practice quiets my mind and allows me to feel completely peaceful and blissful.

6. Surround yourself with positive people: Look at the people you are spending time with and ask yourself whether these people are nurturing your well-being.

Although happiness is an inward process, we are all very affected by those we spend time with. Just as you would not pick rotten fruit and vegetables at the supermarket, be careful about the people you choose to spend time with.

Remember to disconnect from people and situations that are no longer working for you. Find kind and loving people who have the same common interests as you do.

Decide to live! Decide to be happy! Move forward with positive energy to achieve your dreams!

Questions for Reflection

1. What changes do you need to make with your eating and exercising habits so your body will feel better?

2. What affirmations will you tell yourself on a daily basis going forward?

3. What practices or changes can you implement to find greater peace and happiness?

- Chapter 26 -

My Dream of Becoming a Motivational Speaker

There is magic and power in words. The ability to use words to uplift, inspire, and motivate is truly a gift and an art form. There have been great and famous speakers, but the person who first inspired me to become a motivational speaker was my older sister, Vonny.

Vonny was Governor of Girls State, a leadership development event for selected girls from each high school throughout the State of Washington. My father, a traveling salesman, was going to stop and listen to Vonny on his trip to Ellensburg. He invited me to go with him.

We were late as we rushed into the large, dark auditorium. Vonny was already giving her speech. She was talking about attending Garfield High School in Seattle's inner city, which consisted of 98 percent African American students.

She went on to speak about her work volunteering on an Indian reservation. And then she said, "Whether you are from a small town in the middle of wheat fields or a big city, whether you are Indian, African American, or Caucasian, whatever your religion, we are all connected. Our diversity makes us stronger."

The room was quiet; there was not a sound. We were excited, riveted to each word. At the end of Vonny's speech, the girls rose to their feet cheering.

I was truly inspired by Vonny's stories and how words can make a positive difference in peoples' lives, or do the opposite. There is such power in words, in vocal tone, and body language.

As I listened and watched my sister, I felt something stir inside my heart and soul. I knew then that I wanted to become a motivational speaker.

During the next few years, I became very inspired by John F. Kennedy and Martin Luther King, Jr. It was very sad when we lost these two great men.

I wondered what it was about their words that can scare people, instead of opening them up to the great dreams and possibilities for their own lives.

Years later, while working in Seattle, I was invited to attend a Toastmasters meeting. I won Best Speaker for Table Topics (impromptu speaking) and was given a postcard of a lion with the words "Best Speaker Table Topics" handwritten on the card.

I saved that card because it symbolizes for me the beginning of my long and rewarding journey to becoming a public speaker.

At that meeting, what amazed me the most was the way people really listened to what I had to say. There were only ten people in attendance sitting around a table.

That is the same number as the people in my family. When I was growing up, everyone talked at the same time at the dinner table. No one asked what I thought. It was survival of the loudest.

Sometimes there was one pie for dessert that was divided into ten slivers. I always wanted more pie. After I grew up and left home, I bought pies and ate them all by myself. Blueberry, pecan, apple, cherry, rhubarb. Yum!

One day, I realized I was becoming pleasantly plump so I decided it was time to give up that childhood desire for more pie.

At the Toastmasters meetings, someone always evaluates the speeches. They use the sandwich approach, pointing out what is good, then what can be improved, and ending with a positive, encouraging comment.

I knew that at least one person, my speech evaluator, was listening closely to what I was saying. Everyone votes after a speech, and it is really encouraging to win ribbons for Best Speaker, Best Table Topics Presenter, and Best Evaluator.

Getting immediate positive feedback and awards is so encouraging that it motivates us to work harder to achieve our goals.

Each year in Toastmasters, there are statewide competitions for the best humorous speaker and the best inspirational speaker. Later when I moved to Hawaii, I won the state championship twice and placed in the regional championships.

Competing encouraged me to practice, present to as many groups as possible, and get constant feedback. Just like when I practiced the cello for so many years, the more I practiced speaking, the more I excelled.

The process of competing can be challenging. Since everyone wants to win, there is a lot of pressure. One year during the regional contest in San Francisco, the sound system screeched as I began speaking, so everyone covered their ears.

I had to start over. I came in second place. Sadly, because I didn't place first, I was not able to compete in the World Championship of Public Speaking.

After the contest, I decided to go river rafting in Oregon to relax and overcome the disappointment of not winning. On that trip I had a great realization: to achieve our dreams, we must be willing to compete in the world, yet remember to support, to help, to make a difference, and to be in harmony with our fellow human beings.

The River of Life

"Paddle Forward!" our guide yelled as our boat was swept into the next rapid on the river. For a few thrilling seconds, huge waves swept over us and engulfed the boat.

We paddled hard, and with each wave, I giggled uncontrollably—a good match for the uncontrollable river. After a couple of minutes, we were out of the rapids and into calm waters, resting, awaiting the next episode of the river's churning, changing temperament.

What a relief to be a long distance away from the intense competition I had just experienced in the Toastmasters speech competition in San Francisco.

There were eight people in the same competition from the western states who really wanted to win, and I was one of them. Competition implies separateness. Someone always wins, but someone always loses. It's fun if you win, and hard if you lose.

On the river, my rafting companions and I were all together in the same boat; ironically, there were eight of us—all eight of us paddling rhythmically, the success of one, the success of all. If the boat were to flip, we would all swim downriver together.

The water was so clear, pure, life-giving. Everywhere I looked, I saw green trees, lovely plants, frogs sunbathing on warm rocks, and a soaring bald eagle. This awesome place was pristine and stunningly beautiful.

But what happens when our river of life becomes polluted? When we go down a river and everywhere we see garbage and disharmony?

My reasons for giving my speeches were to heal myself and to inspire others. I, myself, had been inspired. By the time I reached the regional competition, my river had become polluted. The desire to win was stronger than the desire to share a special message about life.

On the river, I realized my negativity was a reflection of my own inner feelings, of not feeling good enough just because I exist, of needing outer approval to know I'm okay. I was holding a mirror and seeing my own reflection—one I wasn't proud of.

I wanted to escape those feelings, to stay on the river for the rest of my life, to float, to face the wild rapids and the calm lulling waters, to feel the fresh, cool air seep into my lungs, and exult in the breathtaking beauty.

We took a break for lunch. I told our Indian guide, Alo (meaning "spiritual guide" in the Hopi Indian language), "I never want to leave the river and return to civilization."

He said, "Annabel, the river of life is inside of us. It can be a raging river. Or it can be a gentle, flowing river nurturing plants and animals as it meanders along. You get to choose."

When I got home that evening, feeling exhilarated and totally in love with life again, I thought, *if I don't tell someone about the river, no one will know how it felt. I'll give one more speech so I can tell the world about the river of life.*

I needed to remind myself about those pure river moments. And whenever I talked about it, I remembered.

The night before I competed at the regional competition in San Francisco, I rehearsed my speech in the huge ballroom while workers were setting the tables.

Normally, they would ignore what was going on, but as I gave the speech about my father, it seemed that one by one, each worker stopped, looked up, and watched me as if mesmerized. At the conclusion, there were a few seconds of silence, and then they cheered.

A few days earlier, when I had presented my speech to groups around Honolulu, one man stood up to evaluate my speech. He sobbed uncontrollably. All he could say was, "I wish I could talk to my father one more time."

Another time I gave my speech, three women came up afterwards in tears and wanted to talk about their fathers. We spent an hour together.

Those were the clear fresh moments, touching people's hearts. There was no competition. Only the giver and the receiver. I always felt that I received much more than I gave. How had my river become so polluted that winning became the most important thing rather than encouraging and inspiring others?

Do you ever find yourself forgetting why you are doing something? Does your river sometimes become sluggish and polluted?

Do you find yourself so caught up in winning, in making money, in closing a deal, that you forget about the pure river which gives and gives, nurturing plants and animals without expectation of return?

It is at those times that our river of life has trouble flowing. We aren't getting the results we desire. We feel we are swimming upstream, against the current. Nothing seems to work.

When that happens, in work or in our personal lives, we need to stop, breathe deeply, connect with the greater world of nature, and remember that our purpose is to nurture, to give, to serve, and to create just like the river. Instead of getting stuck, we need to remember the words of Alo, my river guide: "Paddle forward!"

Becoming a Professional Speaker

With my passion for speaking, I decided I wanted to become a professional speaker. I had a list of conventions coming to Hawaii. I called each contact person and asked whether they needed a speaker. One of my first presentations was to the Western Rural Telephone Association at their convention on Kauai.

I lay awake the whole night before. Early the next morning, I gave my presentation to a room full of people. I told my stories without visual aids or sound effects.

Because of that one presentation, five organizations invited me to speak. I flew to Oklahoma, Minneapolis, and Washington, DC. I also spoke in Hawaii. It was a lot of fun and they paid me to speak!

At first, I did not know what fee I should charge. When one CEO who had decided to hire me asked what my fee was, I said, "What are you budgeting for a speaker?"

When he told me, I gasped and said, "You would pay me that much to speak?" He said, "Well...I can pay you less if you prefer." I said, "No, that would be fine."

That was more than twenty years ago. I have now given keynote presentations and workshops to people from all over the world.

As a university professor, I have taught Public Speaking, Business Communications, and Professional Development to students at the undergraduate and graduate levels. My dream of becoming a professional speaker has come true.

Questions for Reflection:

1. How good are you at communicating with others?

2. Would becoming a better speaker and communicator help you achieve your dreams?

3. Did your river of life ever become polluted? How?

4. What have you done to return to your true goals and dreams?

- Chapter 27 -

Helping People Go
Through the Gates

One of the most fulfilling things in life is opening gates for others so they can achieve their dreams. We are all gatekeepers. We hold the keys to others' happiness.

Throughout your life, you will come face to face with people who need your help to achieve their goals and dreams. Will you open the gates for them or slam them shut?

When I was forced out of the organization I worked at, I could almost hear the slam of the door and click of the lock behind me. I was devastated.

However, Jerry Coffee, Kent Keith, and others took their precious time to speak with me. Their encouraging words filled me with a sense of hope, giving me the strength to leave my difficult situation behind and move forward with confidence.

They opened new doors for me to peek through, showing me there were better possibilities and opportunities for me. They truly helped me survive that terrible event in my life.

You can help people in small and large ways. Everything counts. A kind word of appreciation can make a person's day. A smile, a phone call, or a card can make a huge difference.

Listen to others without interrupting. You just never know how much what you say or the little things you do can lift a person's spirit and give them hope.

The big things you do can make a huge difference too. In every organization, there are generous helpers who go out of their way to make people's lives easier. There are also those who seem to resist supporting others or intentionally make things downright difficult. Which person are you?

The guard allowed my father to go through the gate and achieve his dreams of life, liberty, and the pursuit of happiness. How wonderful if we inadvertently help others too.

But being intentional in opening the gates for others is one of the noblest gestures we can make. Be aware of the impact you have on others and be deliberate in treating everyone with the best of intentions.

Minimizing others does not make you a greater person. On the other hand, it requires good character and confidence in oneself to build up and encourage others.

As a motivational speaker, teacher, coach, and trainer, I find great joy in helping people become the best they can be. When people have improved communication skills and renewed belief in their full potential, it is no wonder they can see with more clarity where they can and want to go.

They have a deeper understanding of their own strengths, weaknesses, needs, desires, and what they must do to attain their goals. They contribute to their teams, organizations, families, and society in a richer, more meaningful way.

My hope is that the stories and examples I have shared will help you identify and achieve your dreams. I wish you great success. May you be inspired with new possibilities, and may the gates to your dreams keep opening.

A Final Thought
The Fulfillment of My Dreams

It has been many years since I daringly asked several men if they would consider marrying me and have a baby. It was a risk to be so assertive. I really wanted to have a baby before it was too late. Luckily, one man, Will, said yes. Within a year, we were sharing our wedding vows.

In my life, this one daring act of seeking a husband and a baby has brought me the greatest joy. What if I had never been bold enough to ask? Would I be alone today?

Instead, my husband and son have become two of the most important reasons I am able to deliver motivational presentations today—because I had dreams and took courageous steps. I am forever thankful that I did not hesitate.

Each day, I rejoice in my life, living in paradise, loving Will, Devin, and my wonderful friends, and simply being on this incredible journey.

How about you? Will you take those daring steps to make your dreams a reality?

Never limit your dreams. Do not allow others to squelch your zeal and spirit. Remember to put your dreams to work to make your life more incredible than you ever imagined!

Aloha,

Annabel Chotzen

Annabel Chotzen
Honolulu, Hawaii

About the Author

Annabel Chotzen motivates us with her passion and rejuvenates us with her humor. She empowers us to achieve our goals and then surpass them.

Like her Hawaii homeland, Annabel's strong yet gentle spirit is irresistible. Her enthusiasm is contagious. Her smile is radiant. She inspires people to believe in themselves.

For more than twenty years, Annabel has motivated thousands of people to meet their challenges, to rise above their limitations, and to create transformation in their lives.

Having worked for corporations, government, and entrepreneurs, Annabel understands the challenges of a broad range of organizations and people. She provides practical solutions to real life issues.

An award-winning motivational speaker, corporate trainer, professional development coach and author, Annabel delivers the perfect blend of depth and substance, humor and inspiration. Her ideas are easy to understand, easy to implement, and loaded with long-term value.

Using examples from her own life, Annabel will teach you how to rise above impossible odds, achieve your goals, and then discover that a much higher level of fulfillment has been attained.

Annabel has a Master's Degree in Public Administration from the John F. Kennedy School of Government at Harvard University and a Bachelor of Arts Degree from Bennington College in Vermont.

Annabel has been an Adjunct Professor of Professional Development in the MBA program at Chaminade University. She has taught Business Communications and Public Speaking at Hawaii Pacific University and the University of Hawaii School of Business.

For a description of Annabel's presentations, workshops, and professional development coaching, please visit her website at www.annabelchotzen.com.

Invite Annabel to Provide Speaking, Coaching, Training, and Consulting Services

---

I help build more successful organizations and empower people by delivering keynote presentations, workshops, training, consulting, and group facilitation. I also provide personal development coaching to individuals.

As a consultant, corporate trainer, and award-winning professional speaker, I give people the tools they need to become more effective, productive, and successful.

With a Master's Degree in Public Administration from Harvard University, my areas of expertise include communication skills, employee development, organizational effectiveness, and managing change.

I have a unique gift for identifying key problems and providing solutions to help companies and individuals achieve their goals.

All sessions are offered either virtually or in person. To learn more, please visit www.annabelchotzen.com, email annabel@annabelchotzen.com, or call 808-728-3355.

PROFESSIONAL DEVELOPMENT WORKSHOPS

Being certain that people have the skills and knowledge they need to perform their job at the highest proficiency level is one of the most important aspects of a successful organization.

My training workshops strengthen skills, improve performance, increase efficiency, enhance customer service, and create a more positive environment. A customized program is designed to suit your organizational needs.

Professional development workshop topics include:

- Preventing and Resolving Conflict

- Implementing Effective Communication Skills

- Handling Change in Challenging Times

- Managing Conflicting Personalities in the Workplace

- Building Long-Term Client and Customer Relationships

- Mastering Leadership Strategies

- Delivering Outstanding Customer Service

- Leading and Managing Organizational Change

- Practical Solutions to Deal with Stress, and Burnout

- Coaching Employees for Optimal Results

For more information see
www.annabelchotzen.com/workshops.

PERSONALIZED PROFESSIONAL DEVELOPMENT COACHING

Working with a professional development coach will help you accomplish a higher level of effectiveness and productivity. I provide you with objective insights into achieving your personal and professional goals and dreams.

My coaching sessions directly connect how you spend your time with what you want more of in your life. With my support, guidance, and assistance as an experienced professional and personal development coach, you will gain new perspective and confidence in your life strategies.

Areas of professional development coaching expertise include:

- Achieving Goals and Dreams

- Conflict Resolution

- Handling Change

- Executive Leadership

- Professional Speaking Skills

- Negotiation Strategies

- Time Management

For more information, see www.annabelchotzen.com/coaching.

INTERACTIVE GROUP FACILITATION

When a group or team is having difficulty, bringing in someone who has a fresh perspective can be a good way to create solutions. Utilizing an experienced consultant is a way to provide leadership for the group without relinquishing the reins.

As a facilitator, I will help your group resolve conflict and improve the way it makes decisions. I will teach the people in your organization how to communicate more effectively, overcome obstacles, navigate change, and achieve a much higher level of fulfillment and productivity.

Interactive group facilitation topics include:

• Preventing and Resolving Conflict

• Dealing with Conflicting Personalities

• Improving Communication Skills

• Overcoming Obstacles

• Making Difficult Decisions

• Handling Workplace Change

For more information see www.annabelchotzen.com/group-facilitation.

MOTIVATIONAL KEYNOTE PRESENTATIONS

Hawaii, my home, is a place of extraordinary beauty and gentleness. I incorporate the culture, history, and magnificence of Hawaii into my presentations to give you an unforgettable experience.

I include stunning visual images of erupting Hawaii volcanoes, the powerful ocean, serene mountains, and other images unique to these islands known as paradise throughout the world.

For more than twenty years, I have inspired thousands of people to meet their challenges, rise above their limitations, and create transformation in their lives. My presentations are motivational, educational, and entertaining.

I combine useful skills with uplifting stories and messages. My goal is to impart a deep sense of awakening to the power and courage within you while giving you tools you can use every day to improve your life.

As an award-winning keynote speaker and seminar leader, I customize my presentations to meet the goals and needs of the audience.

After learning about the challenges and issues that your group faces, I will deliver a memorable and life-changing presentation, which is a perfect blend of depth, substance, practical solutions, humor, and inspiration.

Motivational keynote presentation topics include:

- Put Your Dreams to Work

- Handling Change in Challenging Times

- Transforming Workplace Relationships Through Effective Communication and Conflict Resolution

For more information, see www.annabelchotzen.com/keynote-presentations.

BUSINESS CONSULTING

To be competitive in today's marketplace, it is essential for companies to acquire, develop, and fully utilize the skills and unique capabilities of their employees.

Some of the most important and frequently overlooked aspects of operating a business are knowing if employees have the necessary skills and talent to do their job, how well they are performing, and what they need to do their job better.

Along with my husband, Will Hartzell, I provide consulting services for businesses which identify the skills, knowledge, and behavior employees need to be more effective, efficient, and productive.

Business consulting solutions include:

- Facilitate Work Group Interaction
- Training Needs Survey and Report
- Training Plan Development
- Skill Competency Gap Analysis
- Individual Development Plans
- Employee Performance Evaluation
- Competency Management System
- Change Management

For more information, see www.annabelchotzen.com/business-consulting.

Follow your joy, passion, and yearning.
Believe in yourself.
Do what it takes to achieve your dreams.
You are magnificent.
— Annabel Chotzen